RICH DAD'S
BEFORE YOU QUIT YOUR JOB

10 REAL-LIFE LESSONS EVERY ENTREPRENEUR SHOULD KNOW ABOUT BUILDING A MULTIMILLION-DOLLAR BUSINESS

BY ROBERT T. KIYOSAKI

RICH DAD'S

BEFORE YOU QUIT YOUR JOB

**10 Real-Life Lessons
Every Entrepreneur Should Know About
Building a Multimillion-Dollar Business**

By Robert T. Kiyosaki

PLATA™
PUBLISHING

Published by Plata Publishing, LLC

CASHFLOW, Rich Dad, and CASHFLOW Quadrant are registered trademarks of CASHFLOW Technologies, Inc.

  are registered trademarks of CASHFLOW Technologies, Inc.

Plata Publishing, LLC
4330 N. Civic Center Plaza
Suite 100
Scottsdale, AZ 85251
(480) 998-6971

Visit our websites: PlataPublishing.com and RichDad.com

Printed in the United States of America
First Edition: September 2005
First Plata Publishing Edition: October 2012
ISBN: 978-1-61268-050-7

Cover photo credit: Seymour & Brody Studio

Acknowledgments

Entrepreneurship is as much a spirit as it is a calling. It's a fire that burns deep inside, a fire that fuels the leaders among us to defy the odds, hold fast to our dreams, and invent the future.

Before You Quit Your Job is a tribute to entrepreneurs around the world who refuse to back down from their dreams. I acknowledge all those who have inspired me to never lose my passion to be a catalyst of change, to challenge the status quo, and to stay the course.

Thank you.
Robert T. Kiyosaki

OTHER BEST-SELLING BOOKS
BY ROBERT T. KIYOSAKI

Rich Dad Poor Dad
What the Rich Teach Their Kids About Money –
That the Poor and Middle Class Do Not

Rich Dad's CASHFLOW Quadrant
Guide to Financial Freedom

Rich Dad's Guide to Investing
What the Rich Invest in That the Poor and Middle Class Do Not

Rich Dad's Rich Kid Smart Kid
Give Your Child a Financial Head Start

Rich Dad's Retire Young Retire Rich
How to Get Rich Quickly and Stay Rich

Rich Dad's Prophecy
Why the Biggest Stock Market Crash in History Is Still Coming...
And How You Can Prepare Yourself and Profit from It!

Rich Dad's Success Stories
Real-Life Success Stories from Real-Life People
Who Followed the Rich Dad Lessons

Rich Dad's Guide to Becoming Rich
Without Cutting Up Your Credit Cards
Turn Bad Debt into Good Debt

Rich Dad's Who Took My Money?
Why Slow Investors Lose and Fast Money Wins

Rich Dad Poor Dad for Teens
The Secrets About Money – That You Don't Learn In School!

Rich Dad's Escape from the Rat Race
Learn How Money Works and Become a Rich Kid

Rich Dad's Increase Your Financial IQ
Get Smarter with Your Money

Conspiracy of the Rich
The 8 New Rules of Money

Unfair Advantage
The Power of Financial Education

Contents

Contents

Introduction

What Makes Entrepreneurs Different?

One of the most frightening days of my life was the day I quit my job and officially became an entrepreneur. On that day, I knew there were no more steady paychecks, no more health insurance or retirement plans. No more days off for being sick or paid vacations.

On that day, my income went to zero. The terror of not having a steady paycheck was one of the most frightening experiences I had ever experienced. Worst of all, I did not know how long it would be before I would have another steady paycheck. It might be years. The moment I quit my job I knew the real reason why many employees do not become entrepreneurs. It is fear of not having any money, no guaranteed income, no steady paycheck. Very few people can operate for long periods of time without money. Entrepreneurs are different, and one of those differences is the ability to operate sanely and intelligently without money.

On that same day, my expenses went up. As an entrepreneur, I had to rent an office, a parking stall, and a warehouse; buy a desk and a lamp; rent a phone; and pay for travel, hotels, taxis, meals, copies, pens, paper, staples, stationery, legal tablets, postage, brochures, products, and even coffee for the office. I also had to hire a secretary, an accountant, an attorney, a bookkeeper, a business insurance agent, and even a janitorial service. These were all expenses my employer had once paid for me. I began to realize how expensive it had been to hire me as an employee. I realized that employees cost far more than the number of dollars reflected in their paychecks.

So another difference between employees and entrepreneurs is that entrepreneurs need to know how to spend money, even if they have no money.

The Start of a New Life

The day I officially left the company, I was in San Juan, Puerto Rico. It was June 1978. I was in Puerto Rico because I was attending the Xerox Corporation's President's Club celebration, an event recognizing the top achievers in the company. People had come from all over the world to be recognized.

It was a great event, a gala I will always remember. I could not believe how much money Xerox was spending just to recognize the top salespeople in the company. But even though it was a celebration, I was having a miserable time. Throughout the three-day event, all I could think about was leaving the job, the steady paycheck, and the security of the company. I realized that once the party in San Juan was over, I was going to go on my own. I was not going back to work at the Honolulu branch office or the Xerox Corporation.

When leaving San Juan, our plane experienced some kind of emergency. In preparing to land at Miami, the pilot had us all brace, cradle our heads, and prepare for a possible crash. I was already feeling bad enough about this being my first day as an entrepreneur, but now I had to prepare to die on top of it? My first day as an entrepreneur was not off to a very good start.

Obviously, the plane did not crash, and I flew on to Chicago where I was going to do a sales presentation for my line of nylon surfer wallets. I arrived at the Chicago Mercantile Mart late because of the flight delays, and the client I was supposed to meet, a buyer from a large chain of department stores, was already gone. Once again, I thought to myself, "This is not a good way to start my new career as an entrepreneur. If I don't make this sale, there will be no income for the business, no paycheck for me, and no food on the table." Since I like to eat, having no food disturbed me the most.

Are Some People Born Entrepreneurs?

"Are people born entrepreneurs, or are they trained to be entrepreneurs?" When I asked my rich dad his opinion on this age-old question, he said, "Asking if people are born or trained to be entrepreneurs is a question that makes no sense. It would be like asking if people are born employees or trained to become employees?" He went on to say, "People are trainable. They can be trained to be either employees or entrepreneurs. The reason there are more employees than entrepreneurs is simply because our schools train young people to become employees. That is why so many parents say to their child, 'Go to school so you can get a good job.' I have yet to hear any parent say, 'Go to school so you can become an entrepreneur.'"

Employees Are a New Phenomenon

The employee is a rather new phenomenon. During the Agrarian Age, most people were entrepreneurs. Many were farmers who worked the king's lands. They did not receive a paycheck from the king. In fact, it was the other way around. The farmer paid the king a tax for the right to use the land. Those who were not farmers were tradespeople, aka small-business entrepreneurs. They were butchers, bakers, and candlestick makers. Their last names often reflected their business. That is why today many people are named Smith for the village blacksmith, Baker for bakery owners, and Farmer because their family's business was farming. They were entrepreneurs, not employees. Most children who were raised in entrepreneurial families followed in their parents' footsteps and also became entrepreneurs. Again, it is just a matter of training.

It was during the Industrial Age that the demand for employees grew. In response, the government took over the task of mass education and adopted the Prussian system, upon which most Western school systems in the world are modeled. When you research the philosophy behind Prussian education, you will find that the stated purpose was to produce soldiers and employees, people who would follow orders and do as they were told. The Prussian system of education is a great system for mass-producing employees. It is a matter of training.

The Most Famous Entrepreneurs

You may also have noticed that many of our most famous entrepreneurs did not finish school. Some of those entrepreneurs are Thomas Edison, founder of General Electric; Henry Ford, founder of Ford Motor Company; Bill Gates, founder of Microsoft; Richard Branson, founder of Virgin; Michael Dell, founder of Dell Computers; Steve Jobs, founder of Apple and Pixar; and Ted Turner, founder of CNN. Obviously, there are other entrepreneurs who did well in school, but few are as famous as these.

The Transition from Employee to Entrepreneur

I know I was not born a natural entrepreneur. I had to be trained. My rich dad guided me through a process of starting as an employee to eventually becoming an entrepreneur. For me, it was not an easy process. There was a lot I had to unlearn before I could begin to understand the lessons he was trying to teach me.

It was difficult hearing what my rich dad had to say because what he said was exactly opposite from the lessons my poor dad was trying to teach me. Every time my rich dad talked about entrepreneurship, he was talking about freedom. Every time my poor dad talked to me about going to school to get a job, he was talking about security. The clash of these two philosophies going on in my head was confusing me.

Finally I asked rich dad about the difference in philosophies. I asked, "Aren't security and freedom the same thing?"

Smiling, he replied, "Security and freedom are not the same. In fact, they are opposites. The more security you seek, the less freedom you have. The people with the most security are in jail. That is why it is called 'maximum security.'" He went on to say, "If you want freedom, you need to let go of security. Employees desire security. Entrepreneurs seek freedom."

So the question is: Can anyone become an entrepreneur? My answer is, "Yes. It begins with a change in philosophy. It begins with a desire for more freedom than security."

From Caterpillar to Butterfly

We all know that a caterpillar spins a cocoon and one day emerges as butterfly. It is a change so profound, it is known as a metamorphosis. One of the definitions of metamorphosis is, "a striking alteration in character."

This book is about a similar *metamorphosis*. This book is about the changes a person goes through when transitioning from employee to entrepreneur. While many people dream of quitting their job and starting their own business, only a few actually do it. Why? Because the transition from employee to entrepreneur is more than changing jobs. It is a true metamorphosis.

Entrepreneur Books Written by Non-Entrepreneurs

Over the years, I have read many books about entrepreneurs and entrepreneurship. I studied the lives of entrepreneurs such as Thomas Edison, Bill Gates, Richard Branson, and Henry Ford. I also read books on different entrepreneurial philosophies and what makes some entrepreneurs better than others. In every book, good or bad, I found some priceless bit of information or wisdom that has helped me in my quest to become a better entrepreneur.

Looking back at the books I have read, I noticed that they fall into two basic categories: books written by entrepreneurs and books written by non-entrepreneurs. Most of the books are written by non-entrepreneurs—people who are professional authors, journalists, or college professors.

While I have gotten something important from every book, regardless of who wrote it, I did find something missing. What I found missing was the down-in-the-gutter, kicked-in-the-gut, stabbed-in-the-back, terrifying mistakes and horror stories that almost every entrepreneur goes through. Most of the books paint a picture of the entrepreneur as a brilliant, suave, cool businessperson who handles every challenge with ease. The books about great entrepreneurs often make it sound like they were born entrepreneurs, and granted, many of them were. Just as there are natural and gifted athletes, there are natural and gifted entrepreneurs, and most books are written about such people.

Books on entrepreneurship written by college professors have a different flavor. College professors tend to boil the subject to the bone, leaving only the static facts or findings. I find reading such technically correct books difficult because the reading is often boring. There is no meat left, nothing juicy—just the bones.

How This Book Is Different

This is a book about entrepreneurship, written by an entrepreneur who has experienced the ups and downs, the successes and failures, of the real world.

Today, The Rich Dad Company is an international business with products in 42 different languages, doing business in over 55 countries. But it all started as a company that my wife, Kim, and I started in 1997. Our initial investment was $1,500. My first book, *Rich Dad Poor Dad*, has been on the *New York Times* bestseller list for over four and a half years, an accomplishment shared by only three other books. Maybe, as you read this book, it will still be on the list.

Rather than tell you how smart I am at business, which I am not, I thought it better to write a different type of book on entrepreneurship. Rather than tell you how I brilliantly sailed over the tallest peaks and made millions, I thought you might learn more from how I dug many deep holes, fell into them, and then had to dig my way out. Rather than tell you about all my successes, I believe you will learn more from my failures.

Why Write About Failures?

Many people do not become entrepreneurs because they are afraid of failing. By writing about the things many people are afraid of, I hope to help you better decide if becoming an entrepreneur is for you. My intent is not to frighten you off. My intent is to provide a little real-world insight on the ups and downs of the process of becoming an entrepreneur.

Another reason for writing about failures is that humans are designed to learn by making mistakes. We learn to walk by first falling down and then trying again. We learn to ride a bicycle by falling off and then trying again. If we had never risked falling, we would go through life crawling like caterpillars. One of the missing elements I have found in reading many of the books about entrepreneurship, especially those written by college professors, is that they do not go into the emotional trials and tribulations an entrepreneur goes through. They do not discuss what happens to entrepreneurs emotionally when the business fails, when they run out of money, when they have to let employees go, and when their investors and creditors come after them. How would most college professors know how a failing entrepreneur feels? How would they know—since a steady paycheck, tenure, always knowing the right answers, and never making mistakes are highly prized in the academic world? Again, it's all a matter of training.

In the late 1980s, I was invited to do a talk on entrepreneurship at Columbia University. Rather than talk about my successes, I talked about my failures and how much I learned from my mistakes. The young audience asked a lot of questions and seemed genuinely interested in the ups and downs of becoming an entrepreneur. I talked about the fears we all face when starting a business and how I faced those fears. I shared with them some of the more stupid mistakes I made and how those mistakes later became valuable lessons I would never have learned if I had not made the mistakes. I talked about the pain of having to shut a business down and lay people off because of my incompetence. I also shared with them how all my mistakes eventually made me a better entrepreneur, very rich, and most important, financially free, never needing a job again. All in all, I thought it was an objective and realistic talk on the process of becoming an entrepreneur.

A few weeks later, I found out that the faculty member who had invited me to speak at the university was called into her department head's office and reprimanded. His final words to her were, "We do not allow failures to speak at Columbia."

What Is an Entrepreneur?

Now that we have torn into college professors, it is time to give them some credit. One of the better definitions of an entrepreneur is from Howard H. Stevenson, a professor at Harvard University. He says, "Entrepreneurship is an approach to management that we define as follows: the pursuit of opportunity without regard to resources currently controlled." In my opinion, this is one of the most brilliant definitions of what an entrepreneur is. It is bare bones—and brilliant.

The Power of Excuses

Many people want to become entrepreneurs but always have some excuse for why they do not quit their job, excuses such as:

- "I don't have the money."

- "I can't quit my job because I have kids to support."

- "I don't have any contacts."

- "I'm not smart enough."

- "I don't have the time. I'm too busy."

- "I can't find anyone who wants to help me."

- "It takes too long to build a business."

- "I'm afraid. Building a business is too risky for me."

- "I don't like dealing with employees."

- "I'm too old."

The friend who gave me this article by Professor Stevenson said, "Any two-year-old is an expert at making excuses. The reason most people who want to become entrepreneurs remain employees is that they have some excuse that keeps them from quitting their job and taking that leap of faith. For many people, the power of their excuse is more powerful than their dreams."

Entrepreneurs Are Different

Mr. Stevenson had many other bare-bone gems in his article, especially when he compared promoters (entrepreneurs) to trustees (employees), as he labels them. A few of these gems of comparison are:

- **When it comes to strategic orientation**
  Promoter: Driven by perception of opportunity
  Trustee: Driven by control of resources

In other words, entrepreneurs are always looking for the opportunity without much regard to whether they have resources. Employee-type persons focus on what resources they have or do not have, which is why so many people say, "How can I start my business? I don't have the money." An entrepreneur would say, "Tie up the deal, and then we'll find the money." This difference in mindsets is a very big difference between an employee and an entrepreneur.

This is also why my poor dad often said, "I can't afford it." Being an employee, he looked at his resources. Those of you who have read my other books know that my rich dad forbade his son and me to ever say, "I can't afford it." Instead, he taught us to look at opportunities and ask, "How can I afford it?" He was an entrepreneur.

- **When it comes to management structure**
  Promoter: Flat with multiple informal networks
  Trustee: Formalized hierarchy with multiple tiers

In other words, an entrepreneur will keep the organization small and lean, using cooperative relationships with strategic partners to grow the business. Employees want to build a hierarchy, which means a chain of command, with them at the top. This is their concept of building an empire. An entrepreneur will grow the organization horizontally, which means "outsourcing" rather than bringing the work "in house." An employee wants to grow the organization vertically, which means hiring more employees. Formal organizational charts are very important to employees climbing the corporate ladder.

In this book, you will find out how The Rich Dad Company stayed small yet grew big, by using strong strategic partnerships and major publishers throughout the world. We decided to grow in this manner because it cost us less time, people, and money. We could grow faster, grow bigger, become very profitable, have a global presence, and yet remain small. We used other people's money and resources to grow the business. This book will explain how and why we did it that way.

- **When it comes to reward philosophy**

  Promoter: Value-driven, performance-based, team-oriented

  Trustee: Security-driven, resource-based, job-promotion oriented

In simple terms, employees want job security with a strong company, a steady paycheck, and the opportunity for promotion—a chance to climb the corporate ladder. Many employees consider a promotion and title more important than money. I know my poor dad did. He loved his title, Superintendent of Public Education, even though he was not paid much.

The entrepreneur doesn't want to climb the corporate ladder. He or she wants to own the corporate ladder. An entrepreneur is not driven by a paycheck, but by results of the team. Also, as Howard Stevenson states, many entrepreneurs start a business because they have very strong values that are more important than simply job security and a steady paycheck. For many entrepreneurs, their values are more important than money. They are passionate about their work, their mission, and love what they do. Many entrepreneurs will do their work even though there is no money. Rich dad said, "Many employees are passionate about their work only as long as there is a paycheck."

In this book, you will also learn about the three different types of money: competitive money, cooperative money, and spiritual money.

1. *Competitive money* is the type of money most people work for. They compete for jobs, promotions, pay raises, and against their business competition.

2. *Cooperative money* is achieved by networking instead of competing. In this book you will find out how The Rich Dad Company expanded rapidly with very little money, simply by working for cooperative money.

3. A significant part of this book is dedicated to the mission of a business, the values. While we all know that there are many entrepreneurs who are opportunists, working only for competitive money, there are others who build a business on a strong mission, working for *spiritual money*—the best of all money.

Different Styles of Management

There are two other points in the article that are refreshing, especially from a college professor. Howard Stevenson acknowledges that many people say that entrepreneurs are not good managers. Instead of agreeing with this commonly accepted point of view, he writes:

> *The entrepreneur is stereotyped as egocentric and idiosyncratic and thus unable to manage. However, although the managerial task is substantially different for the entrepreneur, the management skill is nonetheless essential.*

Right on, Howard. In other words, entrepreneurs manage people differently. The next point explains why there are differences in management style between entrepreneurs and employees.

Know How to Use Other People's Resources

The other point Stevenson makes correlates closely with his definition of an entrepreneur. The definition is, "Entrepreneurship is an approach to management that we define as follows: the pursuit of opportunity without regard to resources currently controlled." He states, "Entrepreneurs learn to use other people's resources well." This is what causes the difference in management style. Employees want to hire people so they can manage them. It puts them in direct control over them. They will do as they are told or they are fired. This is why employee types want to build vertical hierarchies. They want the Prussian style of management. They want people to jump when they say, "Jump."

Since entrepreneurs are not necessarily managing employees, they need to manage people differently. Very simply put, entrepreneurs need to know how to manage other entrepreneurs. If you say, "Jump," to an entrepreneur, he or she usually responds with some rude comment or gesture. So entrepreneurs are not poor managers, as many people think. They simply have a very different management style because they are managing people they cannot tell what to do, or fire.

This difference in management style also explains why employee types work for competitive money, and entrepreneurs tend to work for cooperative money.

Entrepreneurs Looking for Employees

Some of the more common complaints heard from new entrepreneurs are, "I can't find good employees," or "Employees just don't want to work," or "All employees want is more money." This is a problem for a new entrepreneur with a confused management style. Management style is a matter of training. Again, compliments to Howard Stevenson, a college professor, for getting to the bare-bones differences between entrepreneur and employee.

Don't Wait Until All Lights Are Green

Another reason many people are not as successful as they would like to be is fear—often the fear of making mistakes or the fear of failing.

There is another reason, also a fear, but it appears a little differently. These people disguise their fears by being perfectionists. They are waiting for all the stars to line up before starting their business. They want all the lights to be green before they will pull out of the driveway. When it comes to entrepreneurship, many of these people are still stuck in the driveway with their engine idling.

Three Parts of a Business Deal

One of the best entrepreneurs I have ever known is a friend and business partner of mine. I have formed several companies with him—three that went public and have made us millions of dollars. He believes that there are three parts to putting a business deal together:

1. Finding the right people

2. Finding the right opportunity

3. Finding the money

He explained, "Rarely do all three pieces come together at the same time. Sometimes you have the people, but you do not have the deal or the money. Sometimes you have the money, but no deal or people." He also said, "The most important job of an entrepreneur is to grab one piece and then begin to put the other two pieces together. That may take a week or it may take years, but if you have one piece, at least you've gotten started."

In other words, an entrepreneur does not care if two out of three lights are red. In fact, an entrepreneur does not care if all three lights are red. Red lights do not prevent an entrepreneur from being an entrepreneur.

Anything Worth Doing Is Worth Doing Poorly

Have you ever noticed that software, such as Microsoft Windows, comes in different versions? That means they have improved their product and now want you to buy the better version. In other words, the first product they sold you was not perfect. They may have sold it to you, knowing that it had flaws and bugs and needed to be improved.

Many people fail to get to market because they are constantly perfecting their product. Like the person who is waiting for all the lights to be green, some entrepreneurs never get to market because they are looking for, or working on, perfecting their product or writing the perfect business plan. My rich dad often said, "Anything worth doing is worth doing poorly." Henry Ford said, "Thank God for my customers. They buy my products before they are perfected." In other words, entrepreneurs start and continue to improve themselves, their businesses, and their products. Many people will not start unless everything is perfect. That is why many of them never start.

Knowing when to introduce a product into the marketplace is as much an art as it is a science. You may not want to wait for a product to be perfect. It may never be perfect. It just has to be good enough. It merely has to work well enough to be accepted in the marketplace. However, if the product is so flawed that it doesn't work for its intended purpose, or otherwise does not meet marketplace expectations or causes problems, it can be very difficult to reestablish credibility and a reputation for quality.

One of the marks of a successful entrepreneur is being able to assess the expectations of the marketplace and know when to stop developing and start marketing. If the product is put on the market a little prematurely, then the entrepreneur can simply improve it and take steps to maintain goodwill in the marketplace. On the other hand, delay in introducing a product can mean opportunities irretrievably lost, a window of opportunity missed.

For those of you who remember the early versions of Windows, you'll recall how frequently your computer crashed. (There were some who said that Windows was so full of bugs that it should have come with a can of insecticide.) If an automobile broke down as frequently as Windows did, it would not have been acceptable in the marketplace. In fact, the automobile would have been a "lemon," and the manufacturer would have been forced to replace it. Windows, however, notwithstanding the bugs and the flaws was phenomenally successful. Why was that? It filled a need in the marketplace and was not out of line with marketplace expectations. Microsoft recognized a window of opportunity and started marketing. If Microsoft had waited for Windows to be perfect, it still would not be in the marketplace.

Street Smarts versus School Smarts

In martial arts, there is a saying that goes, "A cup that is full is useless. Only when a cup is empty is it useful." This is true for the entrepreneur.

We have all heard people say, "Oh, I know all about that." Those are words coming from a person whose cup is full. Those are the words coming from a person who believes he or she knows all the answers. An entrepreneur cannot afford to know all the answers. Entrepreneurs know they can never know all the answers. They know their success requires that their cup is always empty.

To be successful as employees, people need to know the right answers. If they do not know the right answers, they may be fired or not promoted. Entrepreneurs do not need to know all the answers. All they need to know is who to call. That is what advisors are all about.

Employees are often trained to be specialists. Simply said, a specialist is someone who knows a lot about a little. His or her cup must be full.

Entrepreneurs need to be generalists. Simply said, a generalist is someone who knows a little about a lot. His or her cup is empty.

People go to school to become specialists. People go to school to become an accountant, attorney, secretary, nurse, doctor, engineer, or computer programmer. These are people who know a lot about a little. The more specialized people are, the more money they make—or at least they hope they make.

What makes an entrepreneur different is entrepreneurs must know a little about accounting, the law, engineering systems, business systems, insurance, product design, finance, investing, people, sales, marketing, public speaking, raising capital, and dealing with different people trained in different specialties. True entrepreneurs know there is so much to know and so much they do not know that they cannot afford the luxury of specialization. That is why their cup must always be empty. They must always be learning.

No Graduation Day

This means the entrepreneur must be a very proactive learner. Once I crossed the line from employee to entrepreneur, my real education began. I was soon reading every book on business I could get my hands on, reading financial newspapers, and attending seminars. I knew I did not know all the answers. I knew I had to learn a lot and learn it fast. Today, nothing has changed. I know that my education as an entrepreneur will never have a graduation day. I will always be learning. In other words, when I am not working, I am reading or studying, and then applying what I learn to the business.

Over the years, this constant study and then application to the business has been one of my most important habits for success. As I said, I was not a natural entrepreneur as some of my friends were. But as in the race between the turtle and the hare, I slowly but surely caught up with and passed some of my friends whose cups became full when they achieved success. A true entrepreneur has no graduation day.

Overspecialized

The following diagram comes from *Rich Dad's CASHFLOW Quadrant*, the second book in the Rich Dad series.

The E stands for Employee.
The S stands for Self-employed, Small business, or Specialist.
The B stands for Big business owner.
The I stands for Investor.

One of the reasons so many entrepreneurs are in the S quadrant rather than the B quadrant is that they are overly specialized. For example, medical doctors in private practice are technically entrepreneurs but may find it hard to migrate from the S quadrant to the B quadrant because their training is too specialized. Their cup is full. For a person to move from S to B, he or she will need more generalized training, and must always have an empty cup.

Here's a side note on the CASHFLOW Quadrant®. One of the reasons why rich dad recommended I become an entrepreneur in the B and I quadrants is that the tax laws are most favorable in those quadrants. The tax laws are not as favorable for employees or self-employed people, the E and S quadrants. The tax code offers greater incentives, or loopholes, for people who either hire a lot of people in the B quadrant or invest in projects the government wants growth in— investments such as low-income housing. In summary, taxes are different in different quadrants.

This book will go into the differences in each quadrant and how an entrepreneur can migrate from one quadrant to another, especially from the S quadrant to the B quadrant.

A List of Differences

Before quitting their jobs, people need to decide if they want to make the transition from employee to entrepreneur. The transition, or metamorphosis, requires a change to some of the following traits.

- A mindset of freedom instead of security

- The ability to operate without money

- The ability to operate without security

- A focus on opportunity rather than resources

- Different management styles to manage different people

- The ability to manage people and resources they do not control

- A focus on team and value rather than pay or promotion

- An active learner—no graduation day

- Generalized education rather than specialized

- The courage to be responsible for the entire business

You may notice that farmers, possibly our earliest entrepreneurs, have had to develop most of these traits in order to survive as farmers. Most had to plant in the spring in order to harvest in the fall. Most had to pray that the weather was in their favor and that pests, diseases, and insects left enough for their family to live on through a long hard winter. Rich dad said, "If you have the mindset and toughness of a farmer, you will be a great entrepreneur."

A Pot of Gold at the End of the Rainbow

While this book starts off describing the process of becoming an entrepreneur as a painful and time-consuming process, I also want to let you know that there is a pot of gold at the end of the rainbow. As with any learning process, even learning to walk or ride a bicycle, the start of the process is always the hardest. You may recall that my first official day as an entrepreneur was not a good day. But if you stick with the learning process, your world will change, just as your world changed when you finally learned to walk or ride a bike. The same is true with entrepreneurship.

For me, the pot of gold at the end of the rainbow has been greater than my wildest dreams. The process of becoming an entrepreneur has made me far richer than I could have become as an employee. Also, I have become somewhat famous and recognized throughout the world. I doubt if I would have become famous as an employee. Most important, our products have reached people throughout the world and in some ways have helped to make their lives a little better. The best part of learning to be an entrepreneur is being able to serve more and more people. Being able to serve more people has been my primary reason for becoming an entrepreneur.

The Philosophy of an Entrepreneur

Becoming an entrepreneur began with a change of philosophy. The day in Puerto Rico that I left the Xerox Corporation, my philosophy shifted from the philosophy of my poor dad to the philosophy of my rich dad.

The shift looked like this:

- From a desire for security to a desire for freedom

- From a desire for a steady paycheck to the desire for great wealth

- From seeing value in dependence to seeing value in independence

- To make my own rules rather than obey someone else's rules

- From a desire to give orders rather than take orders

- A willingness to be fully responsible rather than say, "It's not my job."

- To determine the culture of a company rather than try to fit into some other company's culture

- To make a difference in this world rather than complain about the problems of the world

- To find a problem and turn it into a business opportunity

- To choose to be an entrepreneur rather than an employee

The New Super Entrepreneurs

In 1989, the world went through perhaps the biggest change in history. In 1989, the Berlin Wall came down and the Internet went up. In 1989, the Cold War ended and globalization started to take off. The world went from walls to web, from division to integration.

In his best-selling book, *The World Is Flat*, Thomas Friedman stated that when the wall came down and the web went up, the world went to one Super Power (the United States), global Super Markets, and Super Individuals.

My prediction is there will soon be new Super Entrepreneurs whose wealth will dwarf the wealth of today's mega-rich entrepreneurs. In the 1980s, Bill Gates and Michael Dell were the hot young billionaire entrepreneurs. Then Sergey Brin and Larry Page, founders of Google, and Mark Zuckerburg of Facebook became the hot new billionaire entrepreneurs. My prediction is the next Super Entrepreneurs will not be from the United States. Why? Once again, the answer is that walls have turned into webs.

In 1996, the Telecom Reform Act and money from Wall Street gave rise to such companies as Global Crossing, a bankrupt company that did one important task. It linked the world with fiber optics. Once this fiber-optic network was in place, brainpower from countries such as India did not need to emigrate to Silicon Valley to find work. The brainpower of India could now work from home, for much lower wages.

Due to the power of fiber-optic cables and the Internet, my prediction is that the next Bill Gates or Sergey Brin will come from outside the United States, possibly from India, China, Singapore, Ireland, New Zealand, or Eastern Europe. Brainpower, innovation, technology, and access to the world's Super Markets will create the next teenage multibillionaire or trillionaire entrepreneur.

Today, many Americans are panicked at the idea that our high-paying jobs are being outsourced—shipped not only to India, but all over the world. Today, even tasks performed by accountants, lawyers, stockbrokers, and travel agents can be performed somewhere else in the world for a lower price.

No More High-Paying Jobs

So what does this do to the Industrial-Age advice, "Go to school so you can find a good secure job with high pay," or "Work hard and climb the corporate ladder"? In my opinion, this old Industrial-Age advice is toast. Many employees will have less work to find, much less, since the person competing for their job lives thousands of miles away. Most of us know that wages have not gone up for many workers. How can their wages go up when someone else is willing to work for so much less?

One big difference between an entrepreneur and an employee is that an entrepreneur is excited about the changes that the shift from wall to web is bringing. Many employees are terrified of the changes.

One Last Difference

The last difference I will mention is the difference in pay between employees and entrepreneurs. Some of the most famous CEOs, like Steve Jobs and Warren Buffett, have the lowest salaries.

Could it be because CEOs who are employees work for a paycheck, and CEOs who are entrepreneurs work for some other kind of pay?

Are You an Entrepreneur?

As you can tell, there are differences between employees and entrepreneurs. The purpose of this book is to go deeper into those differences so you can decide, before you quit your job, if being an entrepreneur is the path for you.

In Conclusion

In my opinion, the biggest difference between an entrepreneur and an employee is found in the differences between the desire for security and the desire for freedom.

My rich dad said, "If you become a successful entrepreneur, you will come to know a freedom very few people will ever know. It is not simply a matter of having a lot of money or free time. It is freedom from the fear of fear itself."

"Freedom from the fear of fear?" I asked.

Nodding, he continued, "When you look under the covers of the word *security*, you find fear hiding there. This is the reason most people say, 'Get a good education.' It's not out of the love of study or scholarship. It is out of fear—the fear you won't get a good job or be able to earn money. Look at how a teacher motivates students in school. It is motivation by fear. They say, 'If you don't study, you will fail.' They use the fear of failing to motivate students to study.

"When the student graduates and gets a job, once again the motivation is fear. Employers say, verbally or nonverbally, 'If you don't do your job, you'll be fired.' The employee works harder out of fear— the fear of not putting food on the table or not having money to make the mortgage payments. The reason people crave security is fear. The problem with security is that it does not cure fear. It simply throws a blanket over the fear, but the fear is always there, like the boogeyman chuckling under the bed."

Being in high school at the time, I could really relate to the idea of studying out of fear. "In school, I only study because I am afraid of failing. I do not study because I want to learn. I am so afraid of failing that I study subjects I know I will never use."

Nodding, rich dad said, "Studying for security is not the same as studying for your freedom. People who study for freedom study different subjects than people who study for security."

"Why don't they offer a choice of study in school?" I asked.

"I don't know," said rich dad. "The problem with studying for security is that the fear is always there. And if the fear is always there, then you rarely feel secure, so you buy more insurance and think of ways to protect yourself. You always quietly worry, even if you pretend you're successful and have nothing to worry about. The worst thing about living a life of security is that you often lead two lives—the life you live and the unlived life you know you could be living. Those are some of the problems with studying for security. The biggest problem of all is that the fear is still there."

"So becoming an entrepreneur means you will not have any fear?" I asked.

"Of course not!" smiled rich dad. "Only fools believe they have no fear. Fear is always present. Anyone who says he or she doesn't have fear is out of touch with reality. What I said is, 'freedom from the fear of fear.' In other words, you don't have to be afraid of fear. You don't have to be a prisoner of fear. Fear will not define your world, as it does most people's worlds. Instead of fearing fear, you will learn to confront fear and use it to your advantage. Instead of quitting because your business is out of money, because you are afraid of not being able to pay your bills, being a true entrepreneur will give you the courage to go forward, to think clearly, to study, to read, to talk to new people, to come up with new ideas and new actions. The desire for freedom can give you the courage to operate for years without needing a secure job or a steady paycheck. That is the kind of freedom I am talking about. It is the freedom from the fear of fear. We all have fear. The difference is whether fear causes us to seek security or to seek freedom. An employee will seek security. An entrepreneur will seek freedom."

"So if security is the result of fear, what is the driving force behind freedom?" I asked.

"Courage," smiled rich dad. "The word *courage* comes from the French word, *le coeur*—the heart." He paused for a moment and then finished the conversation by saying, "Your answer for choosing to be an entrepreneur or an employee is found in your heart."

Freedom Is More Important than Life

One of my favorite movies of all times is the classic *Easy Rider*, starring Peter Fonda, Dennis Hopper, and Jack Nicholson. In one of the scenes just before Jack Nicholson is killed, he talks with Dennis Hopper about freedom. I believe it is appropriate to end this introduction with those lines, because it is why I chose to be an entrepreneur. I chose to be an entrepreneur to be free. For me, freedom is more important than life itself.

In this scene, the three of them are camped in a swamp after being teased, threatened, and run out of town by a bunch of good ole boys.

Dennis Hopper: *They're scared, man.*

Jack Nicholson: *Oh, they're not scared of you.
They're scared of what you represent.*

DH: *All we represent to them is somebody who needs a haircut.*

JN: *Oh no. What you represent to them is freedom.*

DH: *What the hell is wrong with freedom, man?
That's what it's all about.*

JN: *Oh yeah. That's right. That's what it's all about all right.
But talking about it and being it—that's two different things.
I mean, it's real hard to be free when you're bought and sold
in the marketplace. Of course, don't ever tell anybody that they're
not free because they're going to get real busy killing and maiming
to prove to you that they are. Oh yeah, they're going to talk to you
and talk to you and talk to you about individual freedom. But
when they see a free individual, it's going to scare them.*

DH: *Well, it don't make them run scared.*

JN: *No. It makes them dangerous.*

Right after this scene, the three of them are ambushed and beaten by the same good ole boys. Nicholson's character dies and Fonda and Hopper ride on, eventually to be killed, not by the same good ole boys, but by other good ole boys who share the same philosophy.

While the movie has different messages for different people, for me, the movie was about the courage it takes to be free—the freedom to be yourself, regardless of whether you are an entrepreneur or an employee.

The rest of this book is dedicated to your freedom.

RICH DAD'S
ENTREPRENEURIAL LESSON #1

A Successful Business Is Created Before There Is a Business

Chapter One

WHAT IS THE DIFFERENCE BETWEEN AN EMPLOYEE AND AN ENTREPRENEUR?

Starting with the Right Mindset

When I was growing up, my poor dad often said, "Go to school and get good grades so you can find a good job with good benefits." He was encouraging me to become an employee.

My rich dad often said, "Learn to build your own business and hire good people." He was encouraging me to become an entrepreneur.

One day I asked my rich dad what the difference was between an employee and an entrepreneur. His reply was, "Employees look for a job after the business is built. An entrepreneur's work begins before there is a business."

99% Failure Rate

Statistics show that 90% of all new businesses fail within the first five years. Statistics also show that 90% of the 10% that survive the first five years, fail before their tenth anniversary. In other words, approximately 99% of all startup businesses fail within ten years. Why? While the reasons are many, the following are some of the more critical ones:

- Our schools train students to be employees who look for jobs rather than train entrepreneurs who create jobs and businesses.

- The skills to be a good employee are not the same skills required to be a good entrepreneur.

- Many entrepreneurs fail to build a business. Instead, they work hard building a job that they own. They become self-employed rather than business owners.

- Many entrepreneurs work longer hours and are paid less per hour than their employees. Hence, many quit out of exhaustion.

- Many new entrepreneurs start without enough real-life experience and without enough capital.

- Many entrepreneurs have a great product or service, but don't have the business skills to build a successful business around that product or service.

Building the Parachute

My rich dad said, "Starting a business is like jumping out of an airplane without a parachute. In mid-air, the entrepreneur begins building a parachute and hopes it opens before hitting the ground." He also said, "If the entrepreneur hits the ground before the parachute is built, it is very tough to climb back into the plane and try again."

For those of you familiar with the Rich Dad books, you know that I have jumped out of the plane many times and failed to build the parachute. The good news is that I hit the ground and bounced. This book will share with you some of my jumps, falls, and bounces. Many of my failures and successes were small ones, so the bounce was not that painful—that is, until I started my nylon-and-Velcro wallet business. I will go into further detail throughout the book because I made many mistakes and learned from them along the way. The success of that business was sky high, and so was the fall. It took me over a year to recover from that powerful bounce. The good news is that it was the best business experience of my life. I learned a lot about business and about myself through the process of rebuilding.

The Crack in the Dam

One of the reasons I fell so hard in the nylon surfer-wallet business was that I did not pay attention to the little things. There is some truth to the age-old statement, "The bigger they are, the harder they fall." My little surfer-wallet business grew so fast that the business was a lot bigger than the capabilities of the three entrepreneurs who created the business. Instead of creating a business, we had created Dr. Frankenstein's monster and did not realize it. In other words, our sudden success was accelerating our failures. The real problem was that we did not know we were failing. We thought we were successful. We thought we were rich. We thought we were geniuses. Even though we consulted expert advisors (like patent attorneys), we did not listen to them.

As three successful entrepreneurs in our late twenties and early thirties, we took our minds off the business and partied into the night. We actually thought we had built a business. We actually thought we were entrepreneurs. We actually believed our own story of success. We started bragging. Champagne started to flow. It was not long before we each had fast sports cars and were dating even faster women. Success and money had blinded us. We could not see the cracks forming in the wall of the dam.

Finally, the dam broke. The house of cards started tumbling down around us. Our parachute did not open.

Too Much Success

The point in sharing my entrepreneurial stupidity is that many people think that it is the lack of success that kills a business. In many cases, that is true. The failure of my surfer-wallet business was a valuable experience because I found out early in my career as an entrepreneur that too much success can also kill a business. The point I am making is that a poorly conceived business can fail whether it is initially successful or not.

Hard Work Covers Up Poor Design

A poorly conceived business startup may be able to survive as long as the entrepreneur works hard and holds the business together with sheer determination. In other words, hard work can cover up a poorly designed business and keep it from failing. The world is filled with millions of small-business entrepreneurs who are able to keep their leaky business afloat with hard work, sheer willpower, duct tape, and baling wire. The problem is, if they stop working, the business breaks apart and sinks.

All over the world, entrepreneurs kiss their families good-bye and head off to their own businesses, their pieces of the rock. Many of them go to work, thinking that working harder and longer will solve their business problems—problems such as not enough sales, unhappy employees, incompetent advisors, not enough cash flow to grow the business, increases in suppliers' prices, rising insurance premiums, increases in landlords' rent, changing government regulations, government inspectors, increasing taxes, back taxes, unhappy customers, nonpaying customers, and not enough time in the day, to name a few. Many entrepreneurs do not realize that many of the problems their businesses face today began yesterday, long before there was a business.

One of the primary reasons for the high failure rate of small businesses is sheer exhaustion. It's tough to make money and keep going when so much of your time is tied up in activities that do not make you any money or that cost you money without offsetting income. If you are thinking about starting your own business, before you quit your job, you might want to talk to some entrepreneurs about how much time they spend on non-income-producing activities to run their business and how they handle this challenge.

As a friend of mine once said, "I'm so busy taking care of my business that I don't have time to make any money."

Do Long Hours and Hard Work Guarantee Success?

A friend of mine quit his high-paying job with a large bank in Honolulu and opened a tiny lunch shop in the industrial part of town. He had always wanted to be his own boss and do his own thing. As a loan officer for the bank, he saw that the richest customers of the bank were entrepreneurs, and he wanted a piece of the action. So he quit his job and went for his dreams.

Every morning, he and his mom would get up at four o'clock to begin preparing for the lunch crowd. The two of them worked very hard, scrimping and cutting corners in order to serve great-tasting lunches with generous portions at low prices.

For years I would stop by, have lunch, and find out how they were doing. They seemed very happy, enjoying their customers and their work. "Someday we'll expand," said my friend. "Someday we'll hire people to do the hard work for us." The problem was that "someday" never came. His mom passed away, the business closed, and my friend took a job as manager of a fast-food franchise restaurant. He returned to being an employee. The last time I saw him, he said, "The pay isn't great, but at least the hours are better." In his case, his parachute did not open. He hit the ground before he built a business.

Now I can hear some of you saying, "At least he went for it," or "It was just bad luck. If his mom had lived, they might have expanded and gone on to make a lot of money," or "How can you criticize such good hardworking people?" And I agree with these sentiments. My intent is not to criticize them. Although not related to them, I loved the two of them dearly. I knew they were happy, yet it pained me to see them work so hard and not get ahead, day after day.

I only relate this story to make the same point. The business began to fail before there was a *business*. It was poorly conceived before he quit his job.

Is Being an Entrepreneur for You?

If this story about working long hours, or failing if unsuccessful and possibly failing if successful, or jumping out of a plane without a parachute and bouncing frightens you, then being an entrepreneur may not be for you.

But if the stories intrigue you or challenge you, then read on. After finishing this book, at least you will have a better idea of what entrepreneurs need to know to succeed. You will also have a better understanding of how to create, design, and build a business that grows with or without you, and possibly makes you rich beyond your wildest dreams. After all, if you are going to jump out of a plane without a parachute, you might as well win big if you are going to win at all.

The Job of an Entrepreneur

An entrepreneur's most important job begins before there is a business or employees. The job of an entrepreneur is to design a business that can:

- grow,

- employ many people,

- add value to its customers,

- be a responsible corporate citizen,

- bring prosperity to all those who work on the business,

- be charitable, and

- eventually no longer need the entrepreneur.

Before there is a business, a successful entrepreneur is designing this type of business in his or her mind's eye. According to my rich dad, this is the job of a true entrepreneur.

Failure Leads to Success

After one of my demoralizing business failures, I went to rich dad and asked, "So what did I do wrong? I thought I designed it well."

"Obviously you didn't," rich dad said with a smirk.

"How many times do I have to do this? I'm the biggest failure I know."

Rich dad said, "Losers quit when they fail. Winners fail until they succeed." Shuffling the papers at his desk for a moment, he then looked up at me and said, "The world is filled with wannabe entrepreneurs. They sit behind desks, have important-sounding titles like vice-president, branch manager, or supervisor, and some even take home a decent paycheck. These wannabe entrepreneurs dream of someday starting their own business empire. Maybe someday some of them will. Yet I believe most will never make the leap. Most will have some excuse, some rationalization, such as, 'When the kids are grown,' or 'I'll go back to school first,' or 'When I have enough money saved.'"

"But they never jump from the plane," I said, finishing his thoughts. Rich dad nodded.

What Kind of Entrepreneur Do You Want to Be?

Rich dad went on to explain that the world is filled with different types of entrepreneurs. There are entrepreneurs who are big and small, rich and poor, honest and crooked, for-profit and not-for-profit, saint and sinner, small-town and international, successful and failing. He said, "The word *entrepreneur* is a big word, and it means different things to different people."

The CASHFLOW Quadrant®

As I mentioned in the introduction, the CASHFLOW Quadrant® explains that there are four different types of people who make up the world of business. They are often different people technically, emotionally, and mentally.

E stands for Employee.
S stands for Self-employed or Small business owner.
B stands for Big business owner.
I stands for Investor.

For example, employees will always say the same words, whether they are the president of the company or the janitor. An employee always says, "I'm looking for a safe secure job with benefits." The operative words are *safe* and *secure*. In other words, the emotion of fear often keeps them boxed in that quadrant. If they want to change quadrants, not only are there skills and technical things to learn, but in many cases they also have emotional challenges to overcome.

A person in the S quadrant may say, "If you want it done right, do it yourself." In many cases, this person's challenge is learning to trust other people to do a better job than he or she can. This lack of trust often keeps them small since it's hard to grow a business without eventually trusting other people. If S-quadrant people do grow, they often grow as a partnership, which in many cases is a group of S's binding together to do the same job.

B-quadrant people are always looking for good people and good business systems. They do not necessarily want to do the work themselves. They want to build a business to do the work. A true B-quadrant entrepreneur can grow his or her business all over the world. An S-quadrant entrepreneur is often restricted to a small area, an area he or she can personally control. Of course, there are always exceptions.

I-quadrant people, investors, are looking for smart S's or B's to take care of their money and grow it.

Rich dad trained his son and me to first build a successful S-quadrant business that had the capability of expanding into a successful B-quadrant business. That is what this book is about.

What Kind of Business Do You Want to Build?

As part of my entrepreneurial training with rich dad, he encouraged his son and me to go out and study as many different types of business systems as we could. He said, "How can you be an entrepreneur designing a business if you do not know about the different types of businesses and entrepreneurs?"

Self-Employed Entrepreneurs

Rich dad was adamant in explaining that many entrepreneurs are not business owners, but self-employed entrepreneurs who own a job, not a business. He said, "You are probably self-employed if your name is the name of the business, if your income stops if you stop working, if clients come to see you, or your employees call you if there is a problem. You may also be self-employed if you are the smartest, most talented, or the best-educated person in your business."

He had nothing against self-employed entrepreneurs. He simply wanted us to know the difference between entrepreneurs who own businesses and those who own jobs. Consultants, musicians, actors, cleaning people, restaurant owners, small-shop owners, and most small-business people fall into the S quadrant and own jobs instead of businesses.

The main point rich dad was making about the difference between a self-employed entrepreneur and a big-business entrepreneur is that many self-employed businesses have a tough time growing into a big business. In other words, they have a real challenge going from the S quadrant to the B quadrant. Why? Again, the answer is that the business was poorly designed before there was a business. It was doomed before it even started.

Rich dad himself started out as a self-employed entrepreneur in the S quadrant. Yet in his mind, he was designing a very large business, run by people much smarter and more capable. Before he started his business, he designed his S-quadrant business to be able to grow into the B quadrant.

Professionals and Tradespeople

He also wanted us to know that many professional people such as doctors, lawyers, accountants, architects, plumbers, and electricians start a self-employed style of business based on a profession or a technical trade. Many of these professions and trades require government licenses to operate.

Also included in this category are professional salespeople, many of whom are licensed independent consultants, such as real estate, insurance, and securities salespeople. Many of these types of people are technically self-employed entrepreneurs, aka independent contractors.

The problem with this type of business is that there is not really a business to sell because there really isn't a business outside of the individual owner. In many cases, there really isn't an asset. The business owner is the asset. If he or she does sell, he or she will not typically get the higher multiples a true B-quadrant business can command. In addition, he or she may have to agree to stay on for the successful continuation of the business. In essence, they go from being the owner to the buyer's employee.

In my rich dad's mind, it made no sense to work hard and not build an asset. This is why he advised his son and me against ever wanting to become employees. He said, "Why work hard and build nothing?"

Later in this book, we will go into some ways this type of entrepreneur can create a business asset—an asset they can build and maybe sell someday.

Mom and Pop Operations

A very large category of entrepreneurs is often referred to as Mom-and-Pop businesses. This type of business gets its name because many small businesses are family businesses. As an example, my mom's mother owned a little convenience store that the family took turns working in.

The challenge for growth in a Mom-and-Pop operation is nepotism. Many people put their children in charge of the business, even though their children may be incompetent, because "blood is thicker than water." Often, the children don't share the passion for the business that their parents had or they don't have the entrepreneurial drive to lead the business.

Franchises

A franchise, such as McDonald's, is in theory a turnkey operation. The entrepreneur sells a ready-made business to a person who does not want to go through the creative and development phase of starting a business. It's like being an instant entrepreneur. One advantage to some franchises is that banks are more inclined to lend money to someone who wants to buy a franchise than to a person who wants to start a business from scratch. The banks are more comfortable with the successful track record of similar franchises, and the banks value the mentoring programs that most franchises have to assist the new entrepreneur.

One of the biggest problems with big-name franchises is that they are generally more expensive to get into and have little flexibility for a budding entrepreneur. Franchises are the type of businesses that typically face legal issues and often end up in court. These fights are some of the most vicious fights in the business world.

Reportedly, one of the main reasons for fighting is that people who buy a franchise business do not want to run it the way the franchisor, the person who created the business, wants them to run it. Also, if the franchise does not do well financially, the franchisee may want to blame the franchisor for the lack of business success. If you do not want to follow the directions of the franchisor to a tee, it is best you design, create, and start your own business.

Network Marketing and Direct Sales

The network-marketing and direct-sales industry is recognized by many to be the fastest-growing business model in the world today. It is also the most controversial. Many people still have a negative reaction, claiming that many network-marketing organizations are pyramid schemes. Yet in reality, the biggest pyramid scheme in the world is the traditional big-business corporation, with one person at the top and all the workers below.

Everyone who wants to be an entrepreneur should take a look at a network-marketing business. Some of the biggest Fortune 500 companies distribute their products through a network-marketing or direct-sales system.

I am not a member of any one network-marketing or direct-marketing business, but I do speak favorably of the industry. People who want to be entrepreneurs should consider joining one of these businesses before they quit their jobs. Why? Many of these companies provide essential training in sales, business-building, and leadership skills not found anywhere else. One of the most valuable benefits from associating with a reputable organization is that it teaches the mindset as well as the courage required to become an entrepreneur. You will also become more familiar with the systems required to build a successful business. The entry fee is typically quite reasonable and the education can be priceless. (To further explain the educational value of such types of business, please go to our website, richdad.com, to see two books on the subject: *The Business School for People Who Like Helping People* and *The Business of the 21ˢᵗ Century*.)

If I were starting my entrepreneurial career all over again, I would start with a network-marketing or direct-sales business, not for the money, but for the real-world business training I could receive—training similar to the type of training my rich dad gave me.

Legal Thieves

One of the more interesting discussions Mike and I had with rich dad involved the subject of entrepreneurs stealing from other entrepreneurs. Rich dad used an accountant working for an accounting firm as an example. One day the accountant, who was an employee of the firm, resigned and started his own business with clients he met while an employee of the firm. In other words, the accountant walked out the firm's door, but took the business with him. Rich dad said, "While this may not be illegal, it still is stealing." While this is one type of business design, it is definitely not the kind of entrepreneur he wanted his son and me to be.

Creative Entrepreneurs

The type of entrepreneur he wanted us to be was a creative entrepreneur like Thomas Edison, Walt Disney, or Steve Jobs. Rich dad said, "It is easy to be a small entrepreneur, like a Mom-and-Pop sandwich shop. It is also relatively easy to be an entrepreneur in a trade or a profession, such as a plumber or dentist. And it is easy to be a competitive entrepreneur—someone who sees a good idea, copies the idea, and then competes against the entrepreneur who created the idea." This is what happened to me when I pioneered the nylon-and-Velcro wallet business. Once we created the market and the awareness of this new product line, competitors came out of the woodwork, and my little business was squashed. Of course, I cannot blame them. I can only blame myself because, once again, I designed the business poorly before there was a business.

Even though I took a pounding, rich dad was happy that I was learning to be a creative entrepreneur, rather than a competitive one. He said, "Some entrepreneurs win by creating. Other entrepreneurs win by copying and competing. The riskiest of all types of entrepreneur is the creative entrepreneur, also known as an innovator."

"Why is the creative entrepreneur the riskiest type to be?" I asked.

"Because being creative means you are often a pioneer. It is easy to copy a successful and proven product. It is also less risky. If you learn to innovate, create, or invent your way to success, you are an entrepreneur creating new value rather than an entrepreneur who wins by copying."

Public and Private

The vast majority of large and small businesses are private companies. A large private company is often referred to as a "closely held" company. That generally means a company owned by just a few owners, and ownership interests are not available to the public at large.

A public company is a company that sells shares of the business to the public at large, most often through stockbrokers and other licensed securities dealers. A public company sells its shares on a stock exchange like the New York Stock Exchange and operates under much more stringent rules than private companies.

Rich dad never formed a public company, yet he recommended that Mike and I create one, as part of our development as entrepreneurs. In 1996, at the same time we were forming The Rich Dad Company, I was also an investor and involved in forming three public companies. One company was created to explore for oil, one for gold, and one for silver. The oil company failed even though it struck oil, which is a story in itself. The gold and silver companies did find substantial amounts of the gold and silver they were looking for. Although the oil company failed, the gold and silver companies made the investors a lot of money.

Working on developing the public companies was a great experience. As rich dad suggested, I learned a lot and became a better entrepreneur in the process. I found out that the rules are a lot tougher for a public company. A public company is actually two different companies serving two different customers—the real customers and the investors. A public company also serves two bosses—the board of directors and the government securities agency such as the SEC, the Securities Exchange Commission. I found out about tougher accounting standards and tougher reporting standards.

When I was first starting out as an entrepreneur, rich dad said, "The dream of many entrepreneurs is to see the company they formed listed on the stock exchange." Yet, after the Enron, Arthur Andersen, Worldcom, and Martha Stewart scandals, the rules became tighter and the compliance requirements much more complicated and expensive. The government was breathing down public companies' backs. Building a public-company business wasn't as much fun as I had expected. Even though I learned a lot, made myself and our investors a lot of money, became a better entrepreneur, learned how to design a public company, and was glad I went through the learning process, I doubt if I will ever form a public company again. That type of business is for a different type of entrepreneur. I can make more money and have more fun in small closely held private businesses.

Can Anyone Be an Entrepreneur?

Rich dad wanted his son and me to understand that anyone can be an entrepreneur. Being an entrepreneur is not that special. He did not want the idea of being an entrepreneur to go to our heads. He did not want us looking down on anyone or thinking we were better than other people if we became successful entrepreneurs.

To this he said, "Anyone can be an entrepreneur. Your neighborhood babysitter is an entrepreneur. So was Henry Ford, founder of the Ford Motor Company. Anyone with a little initiative can be an entrepreneur. So don't think entrepreneurs are special or better than other people. Your job is to decide which entrepreneur you most want to be like— the babysitter or Henry Ford? They both provide a valuable product or service. Both are important to their customers. Yet they operate in very different spectrums, different bandwidths of entrepreneurship. It's like the difference between sandlot football, high school football, college football, and professional football."

With that example, I understood the point rich dad was making. When I was in college in New York playing college football, our team had the opportunity to practice with a few players from a professional football team, the New York Jets. It was a very humbling experience. It was soon obvious to all of us on the college football team that, while we played the same game as the pro players, we were playing at a completely different level of play.

As a linebacker, my first rude awakening was trying to tackle a New York Jets running back coming through the line. I doubt if he even knew I hit him. He ran right over me. It felt like I was trying to tackle a charging rhino. I did not hurt him, but he definitely hurt me. That running back and I were about the same size. But after trying to tackle him, I realized the difference was not physical. It was spiritual. He had the heart, the desire, and the gift of natural talent to be a great player.

The lesson I learned that day is that we both played the same game, but we were not playing at the same level of play. The same is true in the business world and the game of entrepreneurship. We can all be entrepreneurs. Being an entrepreneur is not that big a deal. A better question in designing a business is, "At what level of play do you want to play the game?"

Today, older and wiser, I do not have illusions that I would ever be as great an entrepreneur as Thomas Edison, Henry Ford, Steve Jobs, or Walt Disney. Yet I can still learn from them and use them as mentors and role models.

And that is rich dad's entrepreneurial lesson #1: "A successful business is created before there is a business."

The most important job of an entrepreneur is to design the business before there is a business.

Designing Your Business

Most new entrepreneurs get excited about a new product or an opportunity they think will make them rich. Unfortunately, many of them focus on the product or opportunity rather than invest the time designing the business around the product or opportunity. Before quitting your job, it might be a good idea to study the lives of entrepreneurs and the different types of businesses they created. You might also want to find a mentor who has been an entrepreneur. All too often, people ask business advice from people who have business experience as an employee, but not as an entrepreneur.

Later in this book, we will introduce the B-I Triangle™ which outlines what components are required to create any business, regardless if it is big or small, franchise or individually owned, Mom-and-Pop or publicly owned. Once a person understands the different components that make up a business, it becomes much easier to design businesses as well as evaluate good ones and bad ones.

I recommend keeping your daytime job while you start a part-time business—not for the money, but for the experience. That means, even if your part-time business does not make any money, you are gaining something far more important than money—real-life experience. Not only will you learn about business, you will learn a lot about yourself.

RICH DAD'S
ENTREPRENEURIAL LESSON #2

How to Turn Bad Luck Into Good Luck

Chapter Two

DUMB AND DUMBER
GET RICH AND RICHER

My First Business

My first business failed in 1956. I was nine years old.

My second business succeeded in 1956. I was still nine years old. If not for the failure of my first business, my second business would not have succeeded.

Failing as a Strategy

Failing in business early in life was a defining experience. It was instrumental in developing a success strategy for my future. At the age of nine, I started to realize that making mistakes was the best way for me to learn about business. Although I did not make much money, I realized that the smarter I became by failing and learning from those failures, the richer I would become. Today in business, I will often do something, knowing I might fail. Why? Because at the age of nine, I learned that failing was essential to succeeding.

There are two primary reasons why entrepreneurs fail. One is that the would-be entrepreneurs are so afraid of failing that they freeze, and then do nothing. They get up and go to work—always with some excuse why they are not ready to quit their jobs and start their businesses. The usual excuses include not enough money, too risky, the time is not right, kids to feed, and many others.

The second reason entrepreneurs fail is that they do not fail enough. Many small business owners and self-employed business owners succeed to a point and then stop growing. The business plateaus or begins to die. The business reaches a certain size and then fails to grow. Once again, the entrepreneur needs to risk failing before the business can begin growing.

Fear of failing is the primary reason why so many people do not succeed in life or are not as successful as they would like to be. This occurs not only in business, but in all aspects of life. I remember in high school never going on a date because I was so afraid of being rejected. Finally, just before graduating, I asked a beautiful classmate for a date to the senior prom. To my surprise, she said, "Yes." We had a miserable time, but at least I was making progress.

Another Difference Between an Employee and an Entrepreneur

Recently, during a radio interview, I was called "a risk-taker" by a radio host. I replied, "In today's rapidly changing world, the people who are not taking risks are the risk-takers. People who are not taking risks are falling behind."

The program was a half-hour show that regularly interviewed different people from different walks of life. The show could have been called The Secret to My Success. When the host asked me for my secret, I told her about my first business failure at the age of nine and how that failure led to the success of my second business. I then said, "I realized that failing was the way to success."

"You learned this at nine?" the host asked.

"That's correct," I replied. "Like most people, I do not like failing. I hate it. Yet, that business failure early in life gave me a glimpse into the future. I saw my process for success. Some people get ahead by knowing all the right answers. These people generally do well in school. That is not my process. I get ahead by failing. That is why I have started so many different businesses. More have failed than succeeded. Yet the ones that have succeeded have been pretty big successes, like the success of my real estate company, the two public gold- and silver-mining companies I helped found, and The Rich Dad Company. Also, I did not make much money early in my career as an entrepreneur, but now later in life, I make more money than most people."

"So the secret to your business success is being willing to make mistakes and then learning from them."

"Yes. That is my job as an entrepreneur. My job is to set new goals, create a plan, make mistakes, and risk failing. The more mistakes I make, the smarter I become. Hopefully, the company grows and prospers from the lessons learned."

"I'd get fired if I made too many mistakes on the job," replied the radio interviewer. "To me, making mistakes and failing is failing. I do everything possible not to make mistakes. I hate making mistakes. I hate feeling stupid. I must know the answers. I feel it is important to do everything the right way, the way the company tells me to do it."

"And that is why you are a good employee," I replied kindly. "Employees are hired to not make mistakes. An employee's job is to follow the rules, do as they are told, and do their job the right way. If employees want to do things their own way or do not follow the rules or make too many mistakes, they are fired because they are not doing the job they were hired to do."

"So my job as an employee is to not take risks, and your job as an entrepreneur is to take risks, to make mistakes, and to sometimes fail. Is that what you are saying?"

"Yes," I replied. "That difference is the key difference between an entrepreneur and an employee."

"So you take risks. Is that what you do as an entrepreneur?"

"No, not quite," I said, chuckling. "I don't randomly take any risk that comes along. First of all, I had to learn the science of making mistakes and learning from mistakes. Second, I had to learn how to choose the risks I took. The better my skills as an entrepreneur became, the better my judgment at taking calculated risks. Today, I look at taking risks as part of my job. Failing is not fun, but it is necessary for progress."

"So do you like failing?" asked the host.

"No, on the contrary. I hate failing as much as the next person. The difference is I know that failing is part of the process of my businesses success. The moment I fail, I know I am at the point of a breakthrough in learning. It's the point where the new me emerges."

"The new you?" shrieked the radio host. "What kind of hocus pocus is that?"

"Well," I replied slowly, "we have all experienced this 'new me' experience. For example, when we were babies and could not walk, we stood and fell, stood and fell. Then one day we stopped falling and began to walk. The moment we could walk, we were no longer babies. People called us children, not babies. When we learned to drive a car, we became young adults. Each time we learned a new skill, a new person emerged and our worlds changed. That is what I mean by a new you or a new me. We are new because we have new skills and are better able to face a new world."

"So there is a world of difference between an employee and an entrepreneur?" asked the host sarcastically.

"Oh, absolutely," I replied, working hard not to get caught up in her skepticism. "We live in very different worlds because we are very different people. One of us lives in a world that thrives on risk. The other lives in a world that avoids risk. Different worlds, different people."

There was silence for a moment. The host seemed to be gathering her thoughts. "And that is why so many employees do not make it as entrepreneurs?"

"It's one of the reasons, but not the only reason," I said gently. It's not easy transitioning from a world of avoiding mistakes to a world of actively making mistakes."

"But you make it sound easy," said the host. "You seem so nonchalant about failing."

"I never said it was easy, but it does get easier," I replied. "Look, the point is entrepreneurs have a lot to learn and need to learn quickly. They don't have the luxury of a steady paycheck. They must make mistakes and correct quickly. If entrepreneurs avoid making mistakes, or if they pretend they haven't made a mistake or blame someone else for their mistakes, the learning process will overwhelm the entrepreneur and the business fails."

"You have to learn quickly because you're making something out of nothing," added the host. "There is nothing there to support you."

"Especially in the beginning of your development as an entrepreneur. Yet as you get better, you can go from nothing to something very quickly. One of the great joys of being an entrepreneur is the ability to take an idea and turn that idea into a successful business in a short period of time. Centuries ago, alchemists were trying to turn lead into gold. An entrepreneur's job is to turn an idea into gold."

"It's almost money for nothing," said the radio host.

"Almost," I replied. "If you can do that, you'll never need a job. You can go just about anywhere you want in the world and strike it rich. I do business in over 80 countries. One of my mining companies operates in China and the other operates in South America. An employee or a self-employed person's scope of business is often limited to a town, state, or country."

"So it is a different world," conceded the host.

"Yes," I replied. "That is the world of an entrepreneur. If you are good, you are free to travel the world and do business. Most employees need to apply for a work visa before they can work in another country. An entrepreneur may enter a country as a corporation, or form a joint venture with another corporation in that country. Training yourself to be an entrepreneur is developing your potential to access a world of nearly unlimited wealth."

"And to do that, you need to learn to turn your failures into successes."

"That's correct," I replied.

"And what if you fail and lose money?" she asked.

"It's just part of being an entrepreneur. I do not know many entrepreneurs who have not lost money at one time or another."

"But if an employee lost the company's money, the employee would be fired," said the host with an edge in her voice.

"In many companies, they would be," I replied quietly. "My point is that it is the fear of losing money that costs people the most money. They are so afraid of losing, they lose. They settle for a steady paycheck. They may not lose much money in their life, but they lose out on the potential for great wealth."

Truth During the Commercial Break

"I need to take a commercial break," said the host as she shut down the studio. The sound engineer then took over and began to play the commercials that supported the show.

"I've wanted to quit my job for years," said the host, feeling safer in her soundproof room and not broadcasting to the world.

"But you are paid too much to quit," I said, completing her thoughts.

Nodding, she said, "Yeah, that's it. I'm not paid a lot, just enough so I won't quit and go somewhere else. I need my paycheck. My husband and I make a lot of money, but with four kids in school, there is no way we can do what you are talking about."

Although I did not agree with her point of view, I did let her know I understood how she felt.

"So, what would you say to me? How do I break out? I need that paycheck. I need this job, even if it doesn't pay much. I feel I am trapped in a room, with walls that are closing in around me. What can I do?"

Taking a moment to collect my thoughts, I finally asked, "Do you remember the example I used of the baby learning to walk?"

"Yes, I do," said the host. "And once they can walk, the baby becomes a child. And once they learn to drive, they become a young adult."

"And that is how we learn anything in life. We learn by first having a desire for a change. We want something better. You may have enjoyed your work at one time, but now you know it is time for a change. It's time to move on, just as a baby somehow knows it is time to change. It's time to stop crawling. At some magical point in time, the baby knows when the time is right, when it's time to do something different. The baby begins by clinging to something, like a parent's pants leg or the leg of a table. Babies wobble as they are learning to bridge the gap between crawling and walking. They do this repeatedly, and then one day they let go and fall down. The baby failed. Instead of quitting, which is what many adults would do, the baby repeats the process again and again. Then one day, the baby's mind, body, and spirit come into alignment and the baby can stand. Soon after standing, the baby learns to walk. The baby becomes a child."

"Then come bicycles and then come cars," said the host. "Babies become children, and children become adults."

I completed the thought by saying, "Yes, and the process is similar for entrepreneurship. I just happened to start at age nine, failed at nine, and succeeded at nine. You can do the same if you are willing to risk going through your learning process."

"So you are confident in your skills as an entrepreneur?" asked the host.

"No, not really. I am confident in my ability to make mistakes, correct, and improve my business. I am a better entrepreneur today, and I plan on getting better. But no, I am never fully confident in my skills as an entrepreneur, because I do not rest on my laurels or my past successes. I constantly put myself in situations where I am beyond my skills. I am always on edge, always tentative, always testing myself. That is the way I continually get better."

"And that is why you start new businesses even if you fail?" asked the host.

"I start new businesses even if I succeed. That is why I have so many businesses, businesses that run without me. That is my secret to great wealth. Most employees have one job. As an entrepreneur, I have multiple businesses."

"That's why you do not want to be self-employed or run the business."

"Yes, and that is why I am glad I failed at the age of nine. At the age of nine, I learned how to start businesses that run without me. I wrote about those businesses in *Rich Dad Poor Dad*."

"Yes, I remember," said the host. "I just did not get the significance of those businesses. I did not realize those tiny businesses would have such a profound impact on your life."

Nodding again, I said, "I found my strategy for life at the age of nine."

The sound engineer then informed us the commercial break was over and it was time to continue the interview. The host turned on her microphone and said, "We only have a few minutes left, so let's wrap this up. You're telling us that an entrepreneur's job is to make mistakes and an employee's job is to not make mistakes. Is that your message?"

"Yes, it is. At least that is the way I see it. If I am not taking calculated risks, not making mistakes and growing the company, I should be fired. If my employees make too many mistakes, I might have to let them go. That is why I hire smart employees who hate making mistakes. They do their job. I do mine."

"That is why we say to our kids, 'Go to school so you can get a good job,'" said the host. "Schools are training our kids to be employees."

"Yes," I replied. "If you do well in school, you'll probably do well in the corporate world or in government."

"Did you like school?" asked the host.

"Not really," I replied. "I did not do well in school because I made too many mistakes. I was a "C," "D," and on several occasions, an "F" student. So in school, I figured out that since I was already good at making mistakes, I might as well become an expert at making mistakes. That is why I am an entrepreneur, not an employee. I am not that academically smart. No one would hire me for a high-paying job. I don't like following orders, so I'd probably never be promoted. I like changing things and doing things my way rather than doing what I am told to do."

"You would definitely not get a job at this radio station," said the host.

"I might not get a job here, but I do know how to buy this radio station and hire people smarter than me to run it for me," I added with a hint of humor in my voice.

"Okay, we have to wrap this up," said the host. "Do you have any other examples that show that making mistakes and failing are essential to being an entrepreneur? Is there anyone else, another example besides you, that can support this point of view?"

"Oh, sure," I replied. "Thomas Edison was asked to leave school because teachers complained that he was addled or scatterbrained. Later in life, he was criticized for having failed over a thousand times before inventing his version of the electric light bulb. When asked how he felt about failing over a thousand times, he said something to the effect of, 'I did fail over a thousand times. I believe it was 1,014 experiments that failed before we finally succeeded. It takes at least a thousand failures to qualify you to invent a light bulb.'"

"What does he mean that it takes at least a thousand failures to qualify you to invent the light bulb?" the host asked.

"It means, if you or I wanted to invent a light bulb today, instead of just buying one from the store, we would probably fail at least a thousand times before we knew how to make a light bulb."

"So he was labeled a scatterbrain in school and failed a thousand times before inventing the light bulb," said the host. "That means he is an inventor. How does that make him an entrepreneur?"

"Do you know what company he founded?" I asked.

"No, I do not."

"He founded General Electric, one of the most powerful companies in the world. It was originally known as Edison General Electric, one of the original 12 members of the Dow Jones Industrial Average. Of the original 12, only GE has survived to this day. Not bad for an addle-minded scatterbrain who failed a lot."

The interview was over.

Learn from Your Mistakes

My rich dad believed in learning from your mistakes. He did not view mistakes as bad, but simply as opportunities to learn something about business and yourself. He said, "Mistakes are like stop signs. Mistakes say to you, 'Hey, time to stop... take a moment... you don't know something... It's time to stop and think.'" Rich dad also said, "A mistake is a signal that it's time to learn something new, something you did not know before." Along that line of reasoning, he also said,

"Too many people are too lazy to think. Instead of learning something new, they think the same thoughts day in and day out. Thinking is hard work. When you are forced to think, you expand your mental capacity. When you expand your mental capacity, your wealth increases.

"So every time you make a mistake, stop and take the opportunity to learn something new, something you obviously need to learn. When something does not go your way or something goes wrong or you fail, take the time to think. Once you find the hidden lesson, you will be thankful for the mistake. If you are upset, angry, ashamed, blaming someone else for the mistake, or pretending you haven't made a mistake, you haven't been thinking hard enough. Your mental capacity hasn't expanded enough. You haven't learned the lesson. So keep thinking."

Poor Dad's Philosophy on Mistakes

My poor dad, being an educator, had a different point of view on mistakes. To him, making a mistake also indicated you did not know something, but to him, making a mistake meant you were stupid or intellectually challenged. When my poor dad made a mistake, he often pretended he did not make one, denied making one, or blamed someone else for the mistake. He did not view making mistakes as an opportunity to learn and increase one's intellectual capacity. He did his best to avoid making mistakes. He did not view making mistakes as a good thing, like my rich dad did.

Bad Luck to Good Luck

Lesson number two, turning bad luck into good luck, is the second lesson because of the differences I noticed between my rich dad and my poor dad when it came to making mistakes. In my opinion, it was each man's personal philosophy on the subject of mistakes that determined his ultimate success in life.

His First Big Failure

In earlier books, I wrote about coming home from the Vietnam War and having to decide in which dad's footsteps I would follow. I was about 25 at the time, and both my dads were just turning fifty. My poor dad had just lost his bid as the Republican candidate for lieutenant governor of the state of Hawaii. Since he ran for office against his boss, the governor, my dad was informed that he would never work in state government again. So he was unemployed and out of work at the age of fifty.

The problem was, all he knew was the world of education. He entered the academic world at the age of five and did not leave that world until the age of fifty. Out of work, he had to take early retirement. He took his retirement money, entered the world of business as a reluctant entrepreneur, and purchased a big-name ice-cream franchise. He purchased this big-name franchise because he thought it was a cannot-fail business. In less than two years, the cannot-fail franchise failed, and my father was once again out of work and now out of money.

Blaming Instead of Learning

My poor dad was angry, depressed, upset, and blaming the franchisor as well as his partners for the failure of the business and the loss of his money. It was during this period that I understood why my rich dad stressed the importance of stopping, thinking, learning, and correcting. It was obvious from my dad's mental and emotional state of mind that he had gone through many stop signs and was blaming instead of learning. He was continuing to think with the mental capacity of an employee, not an entrepreneur.

Within just a few months of opening his ice cream business, my dad knew it was in trouble. Once friends stopped coming by to buy a cone, the store was virtually empty. My dad would sit there for hours, all by himself, without customers. Instead of taking a moment to stop, think, and ask for guidance, he fired his employees to reduce costs, worked longer and harder in the business, fought with his partners, and then spent the remainder of his money by hiring an attorney to go after the franchisor. In other words, he used up his money blaming the franchisor for his problems. Out of money, the business finally closed. It was obvious that my real dad had taken bad luck and turned it into more bad luck. Instead of stopping, learning, and correcting, he could not admit that he might be making mistakes. Instead of making things better, he made matters worse.

With his political campaign loss and the loss of his first and only business, he remained angry and defeated until he died, nearly 20 years later. That is why this lesson on mistakes, bad luck, and being dumb and dumber yet getting richer and richer is so important to me.

Show Me a Happy Loser

I once heard Vince Lombardi, the famous coach of the Green Bay Packers professional football team, say, "Show me a happy loser, and I will show you a loser." Over the years, I have taken the time to look deeper into the multiple meanings of that statement. On the surface, Vince Lombardi's words seem to mean that people who take losing lightly are losers. I have been that happy loser many times in life, saying such things as, "Oh, it doesn't matter. Winning is not that important to me. It's how I played the game that matters." On the surface, I may have appeared nonchalant or happy about losing, but truthfully deep down inside, I hated losing. In other words, when I pretended to be okay about losing, I was lying to myself.

The more I thought about Lombardi's quotation, the more meanings came to the surface. Some of the other things he might have meant are:

- Nobody likes to lose. Losing is not something we look forward to.

- Losing should inspire winning.

- Some people avoid losing at all costs because it is so painful.

In my opinion, it is the third meaning that caused my poor dad's business failure. For years, he operated in a world where losing, making mistakes, and failing were to be avoided at all costs. As an employee, he was used to and wanted his steady paychecks and guaranteed benefits. To many workers like my dad, security is far more important than opportunity. That is why so many employees, as a personal philosophy, will avoid making mistakes at all costs. One of the reasons my dad failed was simply because he had avoided making mistakes for too long.

High-Speed Learning

In March 2005, my wife, Kim, and I signed up to take Bob Bondurant's four-day formula-one racing school, located in Phoenix, Arizona. Don't ask us why we signed up for it. We just did simply because it sounded fun and exciting. We are not professional racecar drivers and have no intention of becoming professional racecar drivers.

All my life, I loved movies about Grand Prix races and Formula car racing. I envied Paul Newman and his hobby of auto racing. Starting with my very first car, a 1969 Datsun 2000, I have almost always owned high-performance street cars. After the Datsun, I purchased a Corvette, several Porsches, and a Ferrari. My problem has always been that the cars had more power than I had talent. That problem was one of the reasons why Kim, who also owns a very fast Porsche, and I decided once and for all to learn to drive racecars on a racetrack.

From day one of the class, we realized that we had made a mistake. There were two classes. One class was for High-Performance Driving. This is the class we should have been in. In that class were everyday people who simply wanted to learn to drive regular cars at high speed.

The second class was titled Grand Prix Driving, which is the class Kim and I were in. In this class were professional racecar drivers and amateur drivers with years of racing experience. Kim and I did not realize we were in the wrong class until we noticed that the high-performance class was driving high-performance Cadillacs, while we were in the Grand Prix class driving high-performance Corvettes. The thought of asking for a transfer crossed our minds, but we decided hanging out with professional drivers might be a great way to learn a lot faster. But a knot formed in my stomach once we decided to stay with our class. I knew I was about to face some of my greatest fears.

On the morning of the second day, the knot in my stomach was worse. My logical mind was chattering away, trying to find a way to quit gracefully. In the classroom, my instructor came up to me and kindly said, "You're driving too slowly. You need to drive much faster." At that moment, I was ready to quit and I would have, except the instructor then said, "Your wife Kim is catching on. She's driving much faster than you are." Immediately, my male pride kicked in, logic went out the window, and I had no choice. If Kim was driving faster than me, I had to stay.

As a side note, Kim was the only woman in our class of 12 people. She was very excited about passing men.

Burn Out the Fear

For three full days, the knot in my stomach grew worse as speeds kept increasing, turns came faster, and my mind went into sensory overload with all I had to learn and do at high speeds. At lunch on the third day, I finally asked my instructor why he kept insisting I increase my speed. After all, I wanted to drive slowly so I could learn the lessons before adding speed. He smiled and said, "I want you to go fast because speed will burn that fear out of you. Your fear keeps you stuck. You get up to your fear and then back off of the throttle. Your fear is still driving the car. That is why, when you get up to that fear, I want you to go full throttle."

Again, I wanted to quit. Again, I was being told I was not going fast enough. Again, I thought that the way to learn was to practice at slow speeds, not fast speeds. "Look," said Les, my instructor, "you have to trust that there is a Grand Prix driver inside you. If you don't go fast, you'll never meet the driver inside you. I want you to push yourself, push that throttle, so the driver in you comes forward and takes over the car. If I let you go slowly, the coward in you is still driving the car. There is only one way the professional driver can come out and that is by pushing hard on the accelerator. When you go to full throttle, you have to trust that the professional racecar driver in you will take over."

On the fourth day, the knot in my gut was even worse and my mind was coming up with every reason why I did not have to do this course. The fourth day is when the class stops driving the Corvette and gets into Formula One open-wheeled racers. On this day, we had red jumpsuits and helmets on. Being overweight, I had trouble sliding down into the car. It felt like I was sliding into a coffin. I couldn't move. Again, the coward in me almost took over. I wanted to quit. I could hear my mind saying, "You don't need to do this. You don't have anything to prove. You'll never be a racecar driver. Why are you doing this? This is nuts."

In less than an hour, I was happier than I have been in years. I was at home in the car. Suddenly, all three days of lessons, fears, and frustrations clicked and I was driving the car at full throttle. Instead of fear, it was exhilaration. The driver in me had pushed the coward aside and taken over the car.

As we left the class late that afternoon high as kites, one of the students who was in the high-performance sedan driving course instead of the Formula One racing class we were in came over to us and said, "I loved the class I was in, but I really wish I was in your class."

I replied, "That's funny, because up until today, I was wishing I was in your class."

Two Different Worlds

The reason I mention the driving school is not to brag about my new driving skills. I mention it because the school is about a process, a process very similar to an employee becoming an entrepreneur, a process of going from one world to another.

One of the first lessons I learned is that what I need to do on the streets and highways is opposite to what I have to do on the racetrack. For example, on the highway, if you see a wreck directly in front of you, most people step on their brakes. In the driving school, we were taught to step on the throttle.

In the real world, when a car begins to skid, most people step on their brakes. In driving school, we have to know when to step on the brake and when to step on the throttle. In other words, with different skids, there are different responses. Trust me, stepping on the brake is easy. Stepping on the throttle in a skid is hard. It goes against everything I know. In order to do it, I definitely needed to increase my mental and physical capacity. In the normal world of driving, most people are asked to drive at or below the speed limit. In driving school, we were taught to step on the throttle and go beyond our personal limits to speed. Speed and fear definitely increased my capacity.

A Great Curriculum

My four days at the Bob Bondurant High-Performance Racing School were four days of the steepest learning curve I have ever gone through in my life. The learning curves at the racing school were even steeper than the learning curves I went through at the Navy Flight School. Obviously, Bob Bondurant is not only a great Formula One driver, he is also a wonderful teacher. As a fellow teacher, even though terrified most of the time, I did spend a lot of time evaluating his teaching methodology. I was impressed with the curriculum in the classroom and on the track. For four days, he and his instructors kept us going through our fears as well as our mental and physical limitations with a high degree of safety. Once on the track, I did not have much concern for my physical well-being. The primary concern I had was my wife Kim passing me at higher speeds, which she did on several occasions. Physically I was fine, but my ego was severely bruised each time her car flew past mine.

The Entrepreneurial Process

The process of going from street driver to racetrack driver required that I unlearn many things. In other words, the right things to do on the street will get you killed on the racetrack. Also, the smart thing to do on the street, such as slow down, is often the stupid thing to do on the racetrack. The same is true with going from employee to entrepreneur. They are two different worlds and what is right in one world is wrong in the other.

The reason I tell the story of my poor dad's transition from the world of government to the world of entrepreneurship is to illustrate this point—that what he did right in the world of government was wrong in the world of entrepreneurship.

Since a new entrepreneur is creating something out of nothing, it is obvious that mistakes will be made. In order to succeed, a new entrepreneur needs to be committed to going through these steps as quickly as possible.

1. Start the business.

2. Fail and learn.

3. Find a mentor.

4. Fail and learn.

5. Take some classes.

6. Keep failing and learning.

7. Stop when successful.

8. Celebrate.

9. Count your money, the wins and the losses.

10. Repeat the process.

The Dreaded Disease

In my estimation, 90% of wannabe entrepreneurs do not get to step one. They may have a plan, they may have created the perfect business in their head or on paper, but that dreaded disease known as Analysis Paralysis infects them. Instead of going forward, I have seen many wannabe entrepreneurs design and redesign their plan. Or they find some excuse why the time or the plan is not right. Instead of taking action and failing, they work hard at trying not to fail. They enter the world of Analysis Paralysis.

It is impossible to become an entrepreneur without starting a business. It would be like trying to learn how to ride a bicycle without a bicycle or wanting to learn to be a racecar driver without a racecar and a track. My rich dad said, "The main reason to start a business is to have a business to practice on. If you do not have a bicycle to practice on, how can you learn to ride a bike? If you do not have a business to practice on, how can you learn to be an entrepreneur?"

Different Schools of Thought

At the Bondurant High-Performance driving school, the course curriculum did not focus on doing things right. The course focused on making driving mistakes at higher and higher speeds. As our ability to make mistakes and to correct them at high speeds increased, our confidence went up. On the fourth day of the course, I could make a horrible mistake at high speed, lose control of the car in a turn, regain control, get the car back on the track, get back to full throttle, and continue the race. If I had attempted that on the first day, I would probably be in the hospital.

Once again, I mention this driving school because it reflects a contrast in different schools of thought. My poor dad came from the school of thought that focused on the avoidance of mistakes. That is why he was a good employee. My rich dad came from the school of thought that encouraged making mistakes. That is why he was a good entrepreneur.

Dumb and Dumber

This chapter is entitled "Dumb and Dumber Get Rich and Richer" as a tribute to Jim Carrey. For those of you who have ever watched a Jim Carrey movie, you may have noticed that the dumber he is on screen, the richer he becomes. The same is true with entrepreneurship. If you are a person who needs to always look good, sound smart, never make mistakes, and have all the right answers, then being an employee or a self-employed person might be a better path for you.

When I first started out, I looked like the biggest clown in town. My businesses would go up and come crashing down. Soon my reputation as an entrepreneur in the business community of Honolulu was laughable. If not for my rich dad guiding me and encouraging me to learn from my mistakes and go out and make more, I might have quit my process. I found it painful to play Jim Carrey's screen characters in real life.

Yet as the years went on, the mistakes were bigger but not as painful, simply because I was becoming an expert at making mistakes. Instead of running through five or six stop signs, I did stop, think, learn, correct, and expand my capacity as an entrepreneur before going on. Today I can honestly say I am richer than many of my peers, many who did well in school or had higher-paying jobs early in life, simply because I was willing to be dumb and dumber for years. That's part of paying the price to succeed.

Turning Bad Luck into Good Luck

When we were just entering high school, rich dad taught his son and me how to turn bad luck into good luck. At the time, both Mike and I were sinking fast in our sophomore year of high school because we were flunking English. Mike and I were not great writers.

Instead of being upset with us, rich dad said, "Let this setback in school make you stronger, not weaker. If you can turn this bad experience into a good experience, you will be further ahead of your classmates who passed the course."

"But we both have F's on our report cards," Mike protested. "That record travels with us all the way through college."

"Yes, the grade travels with you, but so does the lesson in life. In the long run, this lesson in life can be far more important than your grades if you take this bad incident and turn it into a good incident."

Mike and I were really angry with our English teacher. We were depressed and felt like failures. Looking at us, rich dad chuckled and said, "Your teacher is winning. You guys are losing because you're acting like losers."

"What can we do?" I asked. "He's got the power. He's already flunked us, and the whole school knows it."

"He only has the power to flunk you," smiled rich dad. "You have the power to take your anger and do something even more stupid, like slash the tires on his car, which I suspect has crossed your minds, or do something good, like take your anger and do well in school or do well in football or in surfing. Take your anger and turn it into greatness. Then you will win. If you take your anger and slash the tires on his car, you will take a bad situation and make it worse. You'll probably spend time in jail if you do what you are thinking."

The Power of Emotions

That day rich dad taught us that as humans we have four basic emotions. They are:

1. Joy

2. Anger

3. Fear

4. Love

He also explained that there were many other emotions, but these were the basic ones. Many of the other emotions were combinations of two or more of these basic emotions. For example, sadness is often a combination of anger, fear, and love, and occasionally joy.

He then taught us that each emotion can be used in two basic ways—for good or for bad. For example, I could feel joy and use the joy to go out and drink heavily, which would be using the emotion of joy for a bad purpose. I could also use the emotion of joy and send thank-you notes to everyone who helped me in life. The same is true with all four basic emotions, even love.

Today, I still do not like my English teacher, yet I am grateful that he flunked me. If not for that F, I might not have studied harder to get through college and I might never have become an international best-selling author.

In other words, that F at the age of 15, combined with my first business failure at the age of nine, has made me a millionaire over and over again. Best of all, not only did I learn many lessons about life and myself, but I learned to turn my anger into joy. And I learned that being dumb and dumber can make me become richer and happier.

And that is one of the steps in turning bad luck into good luck. As rich dad said, "If you can turn bad luck into good luck, you will be twice as lucky in love, life, health, and money."

RICH DAD'S
ENTREPRENEURIAL LESSON #3

Know the Difference Between
Your Job and Your Work

Chapter Three

WHY WORK FOR FREE?

The Difference Between Work and a Job

"Do you know the difference between your job and your work?" asked rich dad one day.

Puzzled, I asked, "Aren't they the same thing? Isn't a job the same as work?"

Rich dad shook his head and said, "If you want to be successful in life, you need to know the difference."

"What's the big deal?" asked Mike as he and I shrugged our shoulders and waited for the lesson we knew was coming, whether we wanted it or not.

"What does your dad always say to you about getting a job?" asked rich dad.

Thinking for a moment, I replied, "He says things like, 'Go to school and work hard so you can get a good job.'"

"Does he say, 'Do your homework so you can get a good job'?"

"Yeah," I replied. "He does say things like that."

"So what is the difference between your job and your work?" asked rich dad again.

"I don't know," I replied. "It all sounds like work to me."

"Oh, I get what you're saying," said Mike. "A job is something I get paid for. I do not get paid for work such as my homework. Work is what I do to prepare me for my job."

Rich dad nodded. "That's it. That's the difference between your work and your job. You get paid for a job, but you do not get paid for doing

71

your work." Looking at me, he asked, "Do you get paid for doing yard work at home, or does your mom get paid for doing her housework?"

"No," I replied. "Not in my family. I don't even get an allowance."

"Do you get paid to do your homework?" asked rich dad. "Does your dad give you money to read books?"

"No," I replied a little sarcastically. "Are you saying that my homework is what prepares me for my job?"

"That is what I am saying," rich dad smiled. "When it comes to money, the more homework you do, the more money you earn on your job. People who do not do their homework make less money, regardless if they are an employee or an entrepreneur."

Thinking for a long while, I finally asked, "So is it true that if I do not do my homework at school, I won't get a high-paying job?"

"Yes, I would say that is true," said rich dad. "At least, if you don't do your homework, you will not become a medical doctor, accountant, or lawyer. If you are an employee, it's tough to get promoted and earn more money if you don't have a trained skill or a college degree."

"And if we want to be entrepreneurs, we need to do a different type of homework?" I asked.

Rich dad nodded and said, "Many entrepreneurs quit their job without doing their homework. That is why so many small businesses fail or struggle financially."

"So you're having us do our homework to become entrepreneurs."

"Exactly," rich dad said. "And that is why I am not paying you. Working for me for free is doing your homework. Many employees do not understand working for free. They expect to get paid for anything they do. That is why they fail. They continue to think like employees. They want that steady paycheck."

Lots of Work, but No Jobs

"In many poor parts of town, there is a lot of work to be done, but there are very few jobs," rich dad continued.

Thinking for a moment, I finally repeated what he said. "There is a lot of work, but no jobs?" To me it was puzzling, and I needed to think more about what he said.

"Why is that?" asked his son, Mike.

"Well, one reason is that we are trained in school to look for jobs. If there are no jobs, people are out of work, even if there is a lot of work to do. When a factory closes or moves overseas, it usually leaves behind a lot of unemployed employees."

Rich dad continued to explain, "Employees see no jobs so they do nothing. On the other hand, an entrepreneur sees a lot of opportunity. The entrepreneur knows that the jobs will come if the work is done."

"So they need to be retrained. They need to do their homework," I added. "That's the work that needs to be done."

"That is some of the work," said rich dad. "Look, the point I am making is that too many people confuse work with their job. Too many people expect to get their job training for free. Even if a person has a job, too many employees expect their employers to provide them with training and pay them at the same time."

"They want the company to pay for their education?" I asked. Being a teenager and not having worked in a big company, the idea of expecting to be paid for training was strange to me.

"Many people also expect the government to provide them with job training for free," added rich dad.

"And that is why you say they are poor people," said Mike. "It's more than financial. It is a poor attitude toward the value of education, training, and preparing oneself to have a skill people will pay for."

Rich dad agreed. "I've seen employees attend training classes while keeping one eye on their watch. At quitting time, they jump up and leave the class, even if the instructor has not finished the lesson. Or I've seen employees who are outside, smoking and gossiping; or drinking in the bar and watching sports on TV; or flirting with other workers, rather than attending the class the employer is paying them to attend. That is why so many people do not get ahead in life financially. Too many won't learn anything, even if it is free or if they are paid to learn it. And that applies to both employees and entrepreneurs."

Since I came from a family of government educators who believed in free education, I asked, "Would you explain a little further the relationship between work and jobs?"

Doctors Worked for Free

"Sure," said rich dad. "Medical doctors spend a lot of money and a lot of time learning to be doctors before they get paid as a medical doctor. That is one reason why they earn more money than most people."

"Doctors do their homework before they get paid," Mike added.

Professional Athletes Work for Free

"They certainly did," said rich dad. "But also look at great athletes who earn a lot of money. I do not know of a single great athlete who got paid for practicing their sport. Most professional athletes started young and practiced longer and harder than the average athlete. Most professional athletes practiced for years and put in many hours, long before they got paid. They had to do their homework before they got their jobs as pros."

"That is why you don't pay us," I said softly. "We work for you for free."

Rich dad smiled. "Even The Beatles worked for free before they became world-famous and rich. Like the medical doctor or professional, they paid their dues. They did their homework. They did not ask for a guaranteed record contract, a steady paycheck, or medical benefits before they began practicing."

"I've bought a lot of their records," said Mike. "I've helped make them rich."

"They made themselves rich," said rich dad with a smile. "Doing your homework applies to more than just money. It also applies to your health. Many people are unhealthy because they do not work out."

"They don't exercise," I said, "so they have poor health."

"Notice the word *poor*?" asked rich dad. "Poor financially and poor in health. People who are lazy and lack discipline are often the people with the worst health and the worst wealth."

"So we need to do our homework if we want to become entrepreneurs," I summarized.

"That is why you boys have been working for me for free for all these years. You've been doing your homework to become entrepreneurs. If I were training you to be employees, I would be paying you by the hour."

"So that is why my dad, a government school teacher, got so angry when I worked for you for free," I added.

Chuckling and nodding again, rich dad said, "Your father thinks like an employee. That is why he thinks I should pay you. He does not understand working for free. He does not understand that you are receiving a priceless education. It's just not the kind of education he values. The type of education an employee needs is different from the type of education an entrepreneur requires."

"That is why he thinks you're cheating us," I added.

"I know," smiled rich dad. "Look, years from now, you'll be a lot richer because of what I am teaching you. What you are learning is much more valuable than a small paycheck."

Why a Business Struggles

Before quitting your job, you will need to find out how many different jobs make up a business.

Rich dad said, "Even if a person is a highly successful employee— let's say in sales—that does not mean he or she will be successful in business." The reason he said this was that selling is only one of many jobs required by a business.

His other point was that a struggling business is a business where a job or several jobs are not being done at all or are not being done well. He said, "An entrepreneur may be working hard but only working hard at one job at a time. That is why so many self-employed business owners struggle or eventually burn out from overwork. They may be working hard, but they may not be doing all the jobs a business requires."

The Basic Jobs of a Business

In the third book of the Rich Dad series, *Rich Dad's Guide to Investing*, the B-I Triangle™ is introduced. The B and I refer to the Business and Investor quadrants of the CASHFLOW Quadrant®.

Here is the B-I Triangle that rich dad shared with me.

Rich dad said to me, "If you are going to be an entrepreneur or an investor, fully understanding the B-I Triangle is essential to your success." As a teenager, I did not really believe or appreciate rich dad's respect for the importance of the B-I Triangle. Today I do.

A Great New Product

Many times individuals will say, "I have an idea for a great new product." As you can tell from the B-I Triangle, the product is only the tip of the iceberg.

Before You Quit Your Job

Job Descriptions for a Successful Business

You can think of the different aspects of a business as job descriptions. To be successful, the business needs someone with the skills to fulfill each of those functions. Starting with the product level, you will see the list of jobs required to bring the product to market. In simple terms, *Product, Legal, Systems, Communications,* and *Cash Flow* are technically all the elements required for a business to function successfully. If one or more of these elements is missing or is being done poorly, the business will struggle and often will fail.

When my poor dad's ice-cream business began to fail, it was not because it was not selling a good ice-cream product. In fact, it was a great ice-cream product. In my opinion, the reason the business failed was that my dad was not a good sales or marketing person. He was a great communicator as a speaker, yet he failed to fill the job description known as *communications*.

Taking my poor dad's ice-cream lesson a little further, my dad did not realize that sales and marketing involve more than simply running advertising or being able to sell an extra scoop of ice cream to a customer. His problems began when he thought the brand of ice cream was all he needed for success. His problems began when he rented a cheap location in a remote shopping mall. His ice-cream shop was located in an obscure corner of a so-so shopping mall. That meant he did not have foot traffic or car traffic passing in front of his shop. No one knew where his ice-cream shop was. He thought the brand of the ice cream was strong enough to pull customers in. His business began failing before there even was a business.

He Almost Made It

In retrospect, he did well when it came to choosing a good product. The legal work for the franchise was also done well. The system for making the ice cream was excellent. The franchisor made sure there was a good accounting package as part of the business, so the cash-flow component was covered. There just wasn't enough cash to count. So my dad did a good job in covering four out of the five elements. He almost made it.

77

Where my dad did a poor job was at the communications level of the B-I Triangle™. He did not fully understand the intricacies of sales and marketing. When sales did not happen, the whole business began to fail. Instead of cutting his losses and purchasing a better location immediately, my dad did what many people do when sales decline and cash becomes tight. He cut back on staff. He cut back on advertising. He went cheaper instead of spending more money.

When he did spend money, he spent it on legal bills, blaming the franchisor for his problem. Few things are a bigger waste of money than a lawsuit. Yet that is what happens when people blame rather than learn. Instead of looking at his own actions and taking personal responsibility for the mistake, my dad insisted he was right. Eventually he went broke. There is a poem that describes people who are willing to die being right.

It goes:

> *Here lies the body of Justin Grey.*
> *He died defending his right of way.*
> *He is right.*
> *His case is strong.*
> *But he's as dead as if he were wrong.*

Every time I see people taking their sweet time in a crosswalk, expecting all cars to stop as they cross a busy street, I think of this poem. When I meet people who need to be right, who habitually blame other people when things go wrong, who would rather argue than listen, who know all the answers, or who think they are the center of the universe, I think of this poem. I also repeat this poem to myself whenever I become Justin Grey.

The Triangle of Financial Success

The B-I Triangle applies to more than just the B and I quadrants. Looking at the following CASHFLOW Quadrant®, you can see that there is a B-I Triangle in each of the four quadrants.

For example, if an employee is a receptionist for a business, a well-answered phone is the product of the job. In my opinion, the receptionist has one of the most important jobs in the company. If the receptionist does their job well, the company actually runs smoother. If the receptionist delivers a bad product—for example, by being rude over the phone—then their value to the company goes down. The receptionist should be counseled, retrained, or terminated. I am sure we have all experienced a rude receptionist at one time or another.

The receptionist also has legal rights. If the company violates those rights, the receptionist can take action. The receptionist is an essential part of the entire business system. At home, the receptionist may be the leader of a system known as a home and a family. If life at home is happy, then chances are that the receptionist does a better job at work. If the systems at home are breaking down—such as no heat, no water, leaky roof, or problem family members—the failing systems at home may affect the systems at work.

Since the receptionist is an integral link in the communication of a business, if he or she has poor communication skills, once again the entire business system suffers. Retraining or removal is essential. If the receptionist has loving communications at home, this reflects in the receptionist's life. If communications at home are abusive, it can greatly affect the job performance of the receptionist.

Managing cash flow at home is very important. If the receptionist spends too much money, this not only affects life at home, but may also affect the receptionist's attitude at work. The number-one reason for arguments in a marriage is money. Sadly, many divorces are caused by problems in the cash flow of the family.

An Entrepreneur's Homework

Before quitting their jobs, entrepreneurs should do their homework. That means making sure that the B-I Triangle's five components for their new business are covered.

1. Product

2. Legal

3. Systems

4. Communications

5. Cash flow

If the entrepreneur is weak in covering just one of the five elements, the business may fail, struggle financially, or fail to grow. That is why the lesson in the first chapter is: A successful business is created before there is a business.

A Simple Checklist

A business is far more complex than this overly simplified list of five jobs. Nonetheless, this simple list has served me well over the years. I often use these five jobs as a checklist. Whenever a business begins to struggle, this list of five jobs can help analyze and identify where the problem or problems may lie.

I Have an Idea for a New Product

Whenever someone says, "I have an idea for a new product," this simple checklist can be used to bring some reality to what may be required to bring the product to market. In most instances, the wannabe entrepreneurs give up on their idea because they are not willing to do their homework. They soon realize why a new product is just the tip of the iceberg, or in this case, the tip of the B-I Triangle™.

Why They Give Up

One reason why so many wannabe entrepreneurs give up is that they start to realize they are only trained for one out of the five levels. For example, a creative artist may only be formally trained at product design. An attorney may only be formally trained for the legal level of a business. An engineer may be formally trained for products or systems but not the other levels. A person with a sales-and-marketing degree may only be trained for the communications level. And an accountant may only be prepared for the cash-flow level. When wannabe entrepreneurs look at the five levels, they often realize they have more homework to do before their hot new product makes them rich.

Self-Employed Professionals

Highly educated professional people often have a higher rate of success because their education often prepares them for more than one element. For example, consider an attorney's business in terms of the B-I Triangle:

- **Product:** The attorney is the product. You hire attorneys for the services they have been trained to perform.

- **Legal:** Attorneys are licensed (which protects them from non-licensed competitors). Generally, agreements are in place defining the rights and duties of the members of the law firm and their relative compensations. In addition, most lawyers enter into engagement agreements (letters) to define their relationship with their clients.

- **Systems:** Lawyers are trained to establish business systems for performing services, and for invoicing and collecting payment for those services. Systems for leveraging the expertise of more experienced attorneys are tried and true within the legal profession. For example, to provide for efficient and cost-effective legal research, less experienced, less expensive attorneys will do the initial research to find applicable case law on an issue, which is then provided to a more experienced attorney for analysis. Commercially available software packages are often used to implement billing and collection systems.

- **Communications:** Attorneys understand that to be successful, they need to maintain a good reputation and a good relationship with their clients. Most law firms market through word of mouth, although some are now resorting to advertising. Most people have an understanding of what an attorney does, which means they need to communicate less or explain less.

- **Cash flow:** People expect to pay for an attorney's services. However, this does not mean an attorney can ignore issues of cash flow. Very often services are not invoiced until the end of the month during which they are provided, and clients often delay paying attorneys' fees. It is not uncommon for 90 or 120 days to pass from the time an invoice for services is sent out until receipt of payment. In the meantime, the attorney's payroll must be met and bills paid.

Again, this is oversimplified. Yet it does explain why people such as attorneys, accountants, medical doctors, dentists, plumbers, electricians, truck drivers, cab drivers, and babysitters may have an easier time setting up a business. There is a market in need of their services and willing to pay for their services.

For professionals such as schoolteachers and social workers, the road to becoming highly paid self-employed entrepreneurs may be a little tougher. It can be done, yet it is a sad reality that someone will be more likely to hire and pay money for the services of a self-employed attorney than a self-employed schoolteacher.

One reason why highly educated people such as my poor dad, a schoolteacher, suffer as entrepreneurs is that their professional education does not prepare them for multiple levels of the B-I Triangle™. Many people such as firemen, nurses, librarians, or secretaries are trained to perform essential services, but not the services required by the five elements of a business. Before they quit their job, I strongly recommend they do their homework.

You Do Not Have to Be First

Many people think Thomas Edison was the first person to invent the electric light bulb which helped him found General Electric. The facts are, he was not the first. Records show that he was actually twenty-third on the list of people who invented working light bulbs. So why does history recognize Edison as the inventor, and why did his company become one of the biggest in the world? The answer is found in his life, in the B-I Triangle, and in the five components of a business.

- Edison was born in 1847.

- From ages 12 to 15, he worked on the railroad selling snacks and printing his own newspaper.

- From 15 to 22, he worked for the telegraph company.

- In 1869 at age 22, he received his first patent.

- In 1876, he constructed his own laboratory in New Jersey.

- In 1878, he invented the tinfoil phonograph.

- In 1879, he invented electric light.

- In 1882, he installed a complete electrical system in New York City.

Communications: Raise Money

You may notice that, instead of attending school, from the ages of twelve to fifteen, Edison worked in sales. He would go up and down the train selling candy and a newspaper he printed. He was working on the communications level.

When I left the Marine Corps in 1974, my rich dad said, "You must get a job in sales. Being able to sell is the basic skill of all entrepreneurs." I went to work for the Xerox Corporation and suffered for two years because I was shy and I hated rejection. But by 1977 and 1978, I was consistently in the top five of all salespersons.

Today, I meet many wannabe entrepreneurs who have a great idea for a new product or new business. The problem for most of them is that they cannot sell, which means they cannot raise money. The inability to raise money may be the number-one reason why most wannabe entrepreneurs give up and go back to their jobs.

Cash Flow: Develop Your Ability to Sell

If you cannot sell, you cannot be an entrepreneur. If you cannot sell, you cannot raise money. If the thought of sales terrifies you, get a job at a department store and begin there. Or get a job with a company like Xerox that requires that you go around to businesses and knock on doors. As your courage increases, you may want to try a company in network marketing or direct sales that is willing to train you.

An entrepreneur raises money from:

- Friends and family

- Banks and organizations that support entrepreneurs

- Customers

- Suppliers

- Investors

- Public markets

I have read books about Edison that say his ability to sell allowed him to have a constant stream of venture capital flowing into his projects. They say he was ahead of his time in understanding and integrating the concepts of self-promotion. His ability to self-promote is one of the reasons he was credited for being the first to invent the electric light bulb when, in reality, he was number twenty-three.

Cash Flow: Develop Your Ability to Sell

Typically the person who raises the money, or puts up the money to start the business, owns the lion's share of the business. So learn how to sell and keep learning. For me, learning to sell was much like learning to drive racecars. It was my own fear that I had to overcome.

I am saddened by the fear in the eyes of people who want to be entrepreneurs, but are afraid of selling.

Legal: Protect Your Asset

In 1869, Thomas Edison received his first patent at the age of twenty-two. He was doing his job by legally protecting his asset. Later in this book, I will go into why this step is so important for any entrepreneur.

Systems: Control the Network

By working for the telegraph company, Thomas Edison learned to understand the power of a system. That is why, when inventing his electric light bulb, he was also designing the electrical system that would power his light bulbs. If he had not worked for the telegraph company, he might not have known the importance of this system.

Another word for system is *network*. That is why the richest people on earth control networks such as television networks, radio networks, gasoline networks, network-marketing networks, and distribution networks. A big difference between a small business owner and a big business owner is the comprehension of the importance of a system or a network. Our success at The Rich Dad Company is largely due to network systems. For example, our publisher distributes our books through their network system of booksellers, and our radio shows travel through the airwaves of radio networks.

Do Your Homework

As you can tell, this overly simplifies the importance of making sure that all five components of the B-I Triangle™ are functioning well. Once again, if one or more of the five components is not being done, the business suffers. If an entrepreneur designs a business and forgets one of the five elements, the business suffers or even fails. The business succeeds or fails before there is a business. That is why it is important to do your homework, even if it means working for free.

As this books goes on, we will further develop the B-I Triangle. Before you quit your job, it is important to look deeper into each component of the B-I Triangle. This does not mean you have to be an expert at each level. This does mean that, as an entrepreneur, you do not have just one level. You have five levels. So before quitting your job, spend a little time learning more about each level.

RICH DAD'S
ENTREPRENEURIAL LESSON #4

Success Reveals
Your Failures

Chapter Four
STREET SMARTS VERSUS SCHOOL SMARTS

Good Grades in the Real World

"If I do well in school, will I do well in the real world?" I asked my rich dad.

"That depends upon what you define as the 'real' world."

The B-I Triangle™ became more meaningful to me after my poor dad shut down his ice-cream franchise. He was in his fifties when he took his early retirement money and life savings and lost it all. Instead of rebounding, which many entrepreneurs do after the loss of a business, my dad seemed to go downhill.

Rather than start a new business, he took a job as the head of the teachers union and went after his ex-boss, the governor of Hawaii, demanding better wages and benefits for teachers. Rather than learning from his mistakes and becoming a better entrepreneur, he once again became an employee and an advocate for employee rights.

One reason why he did not rebound was because he was out of money. Instead of learning to raise capital for his next business venture, he just took a job. He went back to the world of employees where he felt more comfortable. In effect, he went back to doing what he knew— working for and saving money—rather than learning something new, such as how to raise money.

My Education Continues

Realizing that it was the lack of skill in the communications level that brought my dad down, I applied for a job in sales at IBM and the Xerox Corporation. It was not the paycheck but the sales training that I was applying for. Rich dad had told me that if I wanted to be an entrepreneur, I had best do my homework at the communications level of the B-I Triangle™.

After two interviews, it was obvious that IBM was not the company for me, and I am certain they knew that I was not the employee for them. After five interviews at Xerox, however, I was on the short list of ten candidates applying for four positions. The final interview was with the Honolulu branch manager. On that day, six of the ten finalists sat outside his office. The other four candidates had already been interviewed.

At the time of the interview, I was still in the Marine Corps and was dressed in my Marine Corps uniform. Sitting outside the branch manager's office, I nervously surveyed my competition. All of them were younger than I was, fresh out of college, very attractive men and women, and dressed like corporate executives.

The Vietnam War was still on and very unpopular in some circles, which meant men in uniform were unpopular in those circles as well. Being off the military base and in downtown Honolulu among civilians was not fun. I had never been spit on, but I was spit at several times. Sitting next to these young people in business attire, I felt really out of place in my Marine Corps uniform, which consisted of a short-sleeved khaki shirt, green slacks, short haircut, and military decorations.

Finally, the secretary notified me that the big boss was ready to talk to me. I entered his office and took a seat in front of him. Reaching across the desk to shake my hand, he wasted no time in saying what he had to say. "I've reviewed your file. You come highly recommended by the rest of my staff who interviewed you. They believe you could be a valuable asset to our sales team."

With that, I took a deep but quiet breath and waited for the good or the bad news. Although he was saying nice things, I noticed that he had trouble looking at me. His eyes were constantly buried in my file folder.

Finally he looked up and said, "I hate to tell you this, but I am going to be the one who turns you down." Standing, he extended his hand and said, "Thank you for applying."

I stood and shook his hand, but my blood was boiling. I wanted to know why. Why was I turned down? Figuring that I had nothing to lose, I asked, "With all due respect, sir, would you mind telling me why you're turning me down? You haven't even given me the courtesy of an interview. Can you give me a specific reason why you're so sure I'm no longer a candidate?"

"Now is not the time," said the branch manager. "At this moment, we have ten excellent applicants and only four openings. I wish we had more openings, but we don't. Why not wait a year and reapply? Maybe your chances will be better then. Now, if you'll excuse me, I need to continue interviewing the other candidates."

Looking directly at him, I said, "Just give me a reason. How can you tell which one of us is better than the other without an interview? Besides, I believe this is a very rude way to treat me. You have me come all the way over here and then do not even have the courtesy to interview me. So just tell me how you can make a decision without an interview. That is all I want to know."

"Okay, if you must know, you are the only applicant without an MBA. You only have a bachelor's degree." With that, the branch manager walked to the door to show me out.

"Just a minute," I said. "After earning my bachelor's degree from the Merchant Marine Academy, I've spent five years in the Marine Corps fighting a war no one wanted to fight. I did not have to go to war because I was sailing for the oil industry. I was employed by Standard Oil which made me draft-exempt, yet I volunteered anyway. And now you're telling me that you are not going to hire me because I didn't go back to college to get my master's degree? I had other things to do. There was a war to fight. And you're telling me that you'd rather hire draft dodgers who went to school?"

"That is not what we are here to discuss. We are not here to discuss the war or our political inclinations," said the manager, who was about my age. "And yes, I am hiring people who went back to school. The job market is tight. We have many qualified applicants so we can afford to be choosy. Right now, we are only hiring applicants with MBAs. That is how we are making our decision. Go back, get your MBA, and maybe then we'll talk."

"So why wasn't I told this earlier?" I asked. "Why let me go through this process only to tell me now?"

"We make exceptions for exceptional people," said the manager. "Even though you do not have a master's degree, our screeners thought you might have other qualities we are looking for. So far, my other managers thought you were good, but not exceptional."

At that moment, I decided to become exceptional—or at least memorable. The manager held the door open and once again extended his hand for a weak handshake with a weak smile. Refusing to shake his hand, I asked in a loud voice, "Tell me something. What does a college degree have to do with sales?" With those words, all the other applicants with their MBAs turned their heads and stared at the open door.

"It shows character. It shows dedication and a high degree of intelligence."

"So what does a college degree have to do with sales?" I repeated.

"Okay," said the manager. "What makes you think you can sell, Mr. Marine? What makes you think you're better qualified to sell than these applicants who have more education than you?"

"Because I have spent five years getting a different kind of education, an education you cannot find in school. While these kids were cramming for college exams, I was flying a helicopter into Viet Cong machine-gun nests. My education has been in leadership, to bring out the best in my troops even though we were all terrified. Not only have we been trained in classrooms to think under pressure, we have had to think under pressure in actual combat. Most important, I have been trained to think of the mission before I think of myself, to think of my men before I think of myself. These college kids have been trained to merely kiss butt for a higher grade."

To my surprise, the branch manager was listening. I had his attention. At that moment, I decided to go for the close.

"Even though I do not have an MBA, I know I have the guts, the courage, and the ability to think under pressure. I know because I have been tested, not in the classroom, but on the battlefield. I know your job is to beat IBM, just as my job was to beat the Viet Cong. For a year, I have been flying my gunship against the Viet Cong, a competitor far tougher and more determined to win than any IBM sales rep. My training for the past five years has allowed me to beat the Viet Cong. That is why, even though I do not have an MBA, my Marine Corps education has prepared me to beat IBM. If you think an MBA program trains these kids to beat IBM on the street, by all means hire them. I have my doubts. But I do not have doubts about me. If I can beat the Viet Cong, I know I can beat an IBM sales rep—even if they have an MBA and I don't."

The entire office area was silent. Looking down the row of hopeful applicants, briefcases carefully placed at their sides or on their laps, I could see the MBAs shaking a little. They heard everything I said.

Turning to the branch manager, I shook his hand and thanked him for listening. I had said my piece. Smiling, I said, "I think I'll go work for your competitor."

"Just a minute," the branch manager said softly. "Please step back into my office. I do have the power to make an exception in spite of our current hiring policy."

Nothing to Lose

After being hired, I went to rich dad's office to tell him the news. I also told him what I said once I heard I was not going to be hired. He smiled and said, "Sometimes we win the most when we have nothing to lose." He also said, "The hard part for most people is getting to "nothing." Most people would rather hang on to a little than let go and get to nothing."

Four Years of Misery

Learning to sell was much harder for me than learning to fly. In fact, there were many days I wished I were back in Vietnam flying against Viet Cong machine-gun nests instead of being on the streets of Honolulu knocking on doors. Basically, I am a very shy person. Even today, parties and social events are painful for me. So knocking on the doors of strangers was a terrifying daily experience.

For two years, I was the worst salesperson on the Xerox sales team. Every time I saw the branch manager in the hallway, I was embarrassed. I saw him, I remembered the Vietnam hero speech I gave to get the job. At my semi-annual reviews, my branch manager always reminded me that he had hired me on faith and how his faith in me was slipping.

Finally, on the verge of being fired, I called rich dad and asked for a meeting. Over lunch, I explained to him that I was failing. My sales numbers were down, my income was down, and I was always at the bottom of the list of salespeople. "What do you think my problem is?"

You're Not Failing Fast Enough

Rich dad laughed his usual laugh. His laugh was his way of letting me know that I was okay and just stuck in the learning process. "How many cold calls do you make a day?" he asked.

"Three or four on a good day," I replied. "Most of the time, I am doing busywork at the office or hiding in some coffee shop, working up the courage to go knock on another door. I hate making cold sales calls. I hate rejection."

"I do not know anyone who likes rejection or making cold calls," said rich dad. "Yet I do know people who have learned to overcome their fear of rejection and the fear of making cold calls. They became very successful people in spite of their fears."

"So how can I stop failing?" I asked.

Again, rich dad laughed and said, "The way to stop failing is to fail faster."

"Fail faster?" I whined. "Are you kidding me? Why would I want to fail faster?"

"If you don't fail faster, you'll fail anyway," smiled rich dad. "Look, you're in the middle of a learning process. The process requires that you make many mistakes and learn from those mistakes. The faster you make mistakes, the faster you get through the process and get to the other side. Or you can quit. Then the process spits you out."

Rich dad was saying the same thing Thomas Edison had said about failing a thousand times before inventing the electric light bulb. Rich dad was saying the same thing my driving instructor was saying to me when I was learning how to drive a racecar at high speed. They were saying that if I wanted to get through the process faster, I had to be willing to fail faster.

Failing at Failing Faster

For a few weeks I took rich dad's advice to heart and did my best to make more cold calls. I knocked on door after door at high speed. The problem was, I was still not getting in front of the person I needed to talk to. Their secretaries were very skilled at keeping pesky salespeople like me away from their bosses.

Now that I was failing at failing faster, I called rich dad again and asked for advice. I called him because I realized I was even failing at failing. Again, he laughed and said, "Keep your daytime job and find a sales job at night. But find a sales job that will let you fail faster."

Naturally I whined and complained. I didn't want to work at night. I was single and this was Hawaii. I wanted to be at the Waikiki nightclubs. I did not want to be selling at night. After listening to me moan and complain, rich dad simply asked, "How badly do you want to be an entrepreneur? *The number-one skill of an entrepreneur is their ability to sell.* If you do not get through this part of the process, you'll be better off as an employee. It's your life. It's your future. It's your choice. You can fail now, or you can fail later."

It was an old lesson. I had listened to the same lesson before. The subject changed—this time it was the subject of sales—but the lesson was always the same. The lesson was that if I wanted to succeed, I had to be willing to fail.

With my own dad's business failure still fresh in my mind, I knew this lesson about sales was especially important. I knew that if I wanted to become an entrepreneur in the B quadrant, I had to learn to sell. But I hated knocking on doors. I dreaded it, day in and day out. One day, after hearing four replies of, "We're not interested," and one, "If you do not get out of my office, I'll call the cops," I hit the depths of depression. I went home rather than back to the office. Sitting in my little apartment in Waikiki, I contemplated quitting. I even considered going back to school and getting my law degree, but I lay down, took a couple of aspirin, and that idea soon passed. It was time to fail faster in a new way.

Working for Free

Rather than find a job at night, I remembered rich dad's advice that it was easier to find work if you were willing to work for free. I found a charity that needed people to dial for dollars at night. Leaving my job at Xerox, I would go uptown and dial for dollars from 7:00 to 9:30 p.m. For two and a half hours, I failed as fast as I could over the phone. Instead of only making three to seven sales calls during the day, I was sometimes making over 20 sales calls in two and a half hours at night. My rejection rate and failure rate went up. But curiously, as my failure rate went up, so did my success in raising money. The more calls I made, the better I became at handling the rejections. I learned what worked with the calls that succeeded and started changing my pitch based on the rejections and the successes. The faster I failed at night for charity, the more I succeeded at Xerox by day. Soon I was climbing up the list of salespeople rather than being at the bottom of the list. Even though I was not being paid at night, my income by day was going up.

Working those extra hours even had an impact on my fun hours. The higher the number of rejections at the charity, the more fun I had in the nightclubs of Waikiki. Suddenly I was not as afraid to talk to the pretty women in the clubs. I was less awkward, less terrified about being rejected. Soon I was even becoming cool and popular, and women were actually hanging around me. After four years at an all-male military school and then years in the Marine Corps, being around so many pretty women was quite a treat. It was a lot better than being the lonely nerd at the end of the bar, staring at the pretty women from a distance.

From 10:00 p.m. to one in the morning, I was the disco duck, just like John Travolta in the movie *Saturday Night Fever*. I even had a white suit, long-collared shirts, disco boots on my feet, and shells around my neck. Everywhere I went, I walked to the sounds playing in my head of the Bee Gees' song, "Staying Alive." My hours were ridiculous and I am sure I looked ridiculous, but it worked. I was failing fast and doing my homework at the communications level of the B-I Triangle™.

Failing Pays Off

In my third and fourth years at Xerox, instead of being at the bottom of the sales pack, I was at the top of the pack. I was also making a lot of money. My failing was paying off. In the fourth year, I was consistently number one in sales. Once I made it to the top, I knew it was time to move on. My school days in sales were over. It was time to learn something new. But little did I know that my success in sales was setting me up for the biggest business failure of my life.

The Four Business Schools

Rich dad explained to his son and me that there are four different types of business schools. They are:

1. **Traditional Business Schools**
   These schools are located at accredited colleges and universities and offer degreed programs, such as an MBA program.

2. **Family Business Schools**
   Many family businesses, such as my rich dad's business, are great places to get a business education—if you are a member of the family.

3. **Corporate Business Schools**
   Many businesses offer intern programs for promising young students. After graduation, the company hires and then guides their career development. In many cases, the company will pay the tuition and even allow time off for further study. After receiving a formal education, promising employees are often rotated through different divisions of the company so they can see the entire business and get hands-on experience.

4. **Business Schools of the Street**
   This is the school that entrepreneurs attend when they leave the security blanket of school, family, or the corporate world. This is the school where your street smarts are developed.

Going to School

All four schools have their merits, their strengths, and their weaknesses. I am not here to say that one is better than the other. In my life, I have been fortunate enough to attend all four, in one way or another.

A Traditional Business School

While at Xerox, I did attend a local university night school with the intent of receiving my MBA. That lasted less than a year. It was not for me. The instructors were either employees of the school or employees of a corporation. The students, for the most part, were seeking to become high-paid, well-educated employees, just like their instructors. They were looking to climb the corporate ladder, whereas I wanted to build and own corporate ladders. It was a different culture and a different curriculum, so I left.

A Family Business School

My friendship with Mike allowed me to attend a family business school via rich dad's businesses. That was a great school for me, simply because it lasted for years. Rich dad was not only a successful real-world entrepreneur, but also a great teacher.

A Corporate Business School

Through the Xerox Corporation, I attended one of the best corporate sales-training programs in the world. Soon after I was hired in 1974, the company flew me first class from Honolulu to Leesburg, Virginia, to spend two weeks at their sales-training facility. It was fantastic. After receiving our classroom training, we immediately hit the streets to practice what we learned in the classroom. Our sales managers were great teachers and mentors. They kept us on track with classroom theory applied to real-world challenges found on the street. We studied hard, not only learning sales skills, but also studying our competitor's products and strategies. We had one objective at that time, and that was to beat IBM. They were tough competitors and a worthy opponent, so we knew we had to be up for the challenge.

The Business School of the Streets

But the toughest business school for me was the Business School of the Streets. Once I left Xerox and hit the streets, I literally hit the streets. The Business School of the Streets was a horrible school, a harsh teacher, and tough on grades. Many times I came face to face with my greatest fears and the depths of personal self-doubt. Yet, it was also the best business school for me. It was just what I needed. Instead of A's and B's as grades, street grades are measured in dollars earned or dollars lost.

Graduation Day

In 1978, I "graduated" from the Xerox corporate business school and entered the Business School of the Streets. It was an emotionally tough transition for me. I went from the world of flying first class, having nice offices, a steady paycheck, and everything paid for by the company, to a world where I paid for everything—including paper clips, travel, and other people's salaries and benefits.

Before I left the corporate business school, I had no idea how much running a business cost. For two years, in order to reduce expenses, my two partners and I did not take salaries. Once again, I was working for free. I knew then why rich dad had insisted that his son and I work for him for free. He was preparing us for the world of entrepreneurship—a world where everyone else gets paid first and you get paid last, if you get paid at all.

Success Reveals Your Failures

Another of rich dad's lessons was "success reveals your failures." In other words, your strengths will reveal your weaknesses. Again, I did not know what he meant until my own business had became successful.

Our nylon surfer-wallet business was successful in two out of the five levels. We were successful at the communications level and the product level. The three partners had trained for years to be successful at those levels. The problem was that we were too well trained at those two levels and our success was too great too soon. It was like hooking up a plastic garden hose to a fire hydrant. As soon as international success put pressure on the system, the whole business blew. Our strong points blew out through our weak points. Our strengths had revealed our weaknesses. Our success had revealed our failures. We had failed to strengthen the legal, the systems, and the cash-flow components of the B-I Triangle™. We had them covered, but we failed to strengthen them as our success increased.

Back to the Drawing Board

After our venture collapsed, two of my partners left the business. I wanted to quit also, but rich dad said, "Rebuild the business. It will be the business school you have been waiting for."

For the next six years, I went back to the drawing board many times. Each failure was less painful, and the recovery was quicker. Each time I failed, I knew what to work on. I knew what I had to study next. The business school of the streets was guiding me. Each failure was actually making me smarter and more confident. Each failure made me less afraid of failing and more excited about learning what I needed to learn next.

Each failure was a challenge, the door to the next world. If I was successful, the door to the next world opened. If I failed and the challenge beat me, the door slammed in my face. If the door slammed in my face, it meant I needed to get smarter. I needed to think harder. I needed to use my creativity to find a way to get into the next door. In many ways, it was like being a salesman on the street again, knocking on doors once more.

When people ask me how we survived through all those years without money, my answer is, "I do not know. I simply took it one day at a time." After my first two partners left and things looked bleakest, two new partners showed up. One of them was my brother, Jon. They brought in some money, but more important, they brought in a new vitality and new skills. One new partner, Dave, brought experience in the systems level of the business. He was excellent at manufacturing. My brother Jon came in to handle the cash-flow level. He was excellent at keeping our creditors happy and suppliers supplying. We also brought in a new advisor, a retired senior auditor from an accounting firm, to help us straighten out our mess. He was happy to work for free since his wife wanted him out of the house anyway. He was happy to have an office to go to. I also believed he found our struggles entertaining. He would chuckle a lot as my two new partners and I moaned and groaned about our problems. More than work for free and straighten out our mess, he also helped us raise more capital by teaching us how to raise capital in a more professional manner.

As I said, we survived by taking it one day at a time. All I knew was that I did not want to go back to a job as my poor dad had done once his ice-cream business failed. In many ways, my philosophy was, "I had gone too far to turn back."

Rich dad was correct. It was the best ten-year business school I could have attended. I started with Xerox in 1974 and finally built a successful business by 1984. It was a ten-year process of building, failing, correcting, rebuilding, and failing. For me, it was the best way to learn. Many times, I felt like I was building a racecar instead of a business. Our team would work on the business, take it out to the racetrack, step on the gas, blow an engine or hydraulic line, and return to the shop.

A System of Systems

In many ways, building a business is very much like building a car. A car is a system of systems. A car consists of an electrical system, fuel system, brake system, hydraulic system, and so on. If one of the systems breaks, the car shuts down or becomes unsafe.

The human body is also a system of systems. We have the circulatory system, respiratory system, digestive system, skeletal system, and more. If one of the systems breaks, the body may also shut down.

In many ways, learning to be an entrepreneur is like going to school to become an auto mechanic or a medical doctor. Just as a medical doctor will look at X-rays or your blood tests, an entrepreneur will look at the B-I Triangle™ to assess the overall health and vitality of his or her business.

After building and rebuilding my nylon wallet business several times, and building and rebuilding other businesses, analyzing businesses became easier and easier. Today, instead of fear, there is excitement. Today, instead of great risks, I see great opportunities. Today I know that if I lost everything,

I could rebuild it. Going through all four of the business schools, and gaining school smarts as well as street smarts, was a great education.

Which Is More Important?

Often I am asked, "What is more important for an entrepreneur—school smarts or street smarts?" Today, my answer is, "Both." To be a successful entrepreneur, you and your team need to be school smart and street smart. When you look at the B-I Triangle™, you can see why. While all five levels require street smarts, the legal and cash-flow components really do require a school-trained professional. Obviously, for the legal level you want an attorney. For the cash-flow level, you want an accountant, preferably a CPA. As obvious as this may sound, you would be surprised how many people come to me wanting advice on how to build a business without an accountant or attorney on their team.

Team Smarts

An entrepreneur needs to know the difference between school smarts and street smarts. More important, an entrepreneur needs to have team smarts, which means finding the best combination of people required by the task at hand. To ultimately win in business, it is team smarts that wins.

In Jim Collins's best-selling book, *Good to Great*, he talks about the importance of having the right people on the bus and in the right seats on the bus. It is also important to get the wrong people *off* the bus. You need to have a team with the talent necessary for all the elements in the B-I Triangle.

Three Big Mistakes

When it comes to legal and accounting professionals, I have noticed three basic mistakes entrepreneurs make:

1. They don't have or don't seek proper legal and accounting advice before setting up their business.

2. They listen to their accountant or attorney too much. Many times I have asked the entrepreneur, "Who is running the business—the accountant, the attorney, or you as the entrepreneur?" Always remember, even if they are smarter than you in certain subjects, you are the one who pays their bills. You need to decide the course of your business.

3. They do not have an accountant or an attorney as part of their team. This does not mean you have to employ them full time. It simply means you need to trust them. They need to know everything and want to know everything. You need to be intimate. Rich dad used to say, "Having a part-time accountant or attorney is like having a part-time husband or wife."

The Difference between School Smarts and Street Smarts

SCHOOL SMARTS	STREET SMARTS
A-Thinker	**C-Thinker**
Analytical skills/critical thinker	Creative thinker/flexible logic
T-Thinker	**P-Thinker**
Technical skills/expertise	People skills/leadership

On the left side are characteristics generally associated with school-smart people. The right side is generally associated with street-smart people. My rich dad said, "If you are to develop as an entrepreneur, you will need to develop all four areas."

I will refer again to these traits, and they should become clearer with each example. For now, I will briefly explain each quadrant:

A-Thinker: We all know people with great analytical skills. They enjoyed solving math problems in school. If you offer a new idea, they will probably be critical or cynical more than open to the new idea. Rather than make a quick decision, they will usually think and analyze the situation for a long period of time before deciding. Before making a decision, they will come back to you and ask for more details.

C-Thinker: We all know people who are creative artists in their work. This does not mean they are artists who paint. It's just that they are creative. They could be accountants or attorneys. They like to see the big picture. They think outside the box. C-Thinkers often drive A-Thinkers crazy. Flexible logic means they are flexible in what makes sense to them. For example, when I say, "I can make more money when the market is crashing," C-Thinkers may be better able to grasp that logic than A-Thinkers. In other words, C-Thinkers can take something illogical and make it fit their logic. They are more open-minded. A-Thinkers often just reject anything that does not fit their way of thinking.

T-Thinker: We all know people who are technical wizards. They may be computer wizards who speak a language found only on Mars. Or they may be motor-heads who think everyone knows how to drop a transmission and fix it. T-Thinkers are often the exact opposite of P-Thinkers. Why? Because T-Thinkers seem to be most comfortable with people who enjoy the same technical subject they do. They attend computer conventions just to meet other computer geeks. They hang out in auto-parts stores just to meet someone they can talk to.

P-Thinker: In high school, the strongest P-Thinkers often ran for student-body officer or were voted Most Popular. Unlike the T-Thinker, P-Thinkers can start a conversation with anyone. At a party, P-Thinkers are the stars. Everyone invites them to their parties because they make the party fun. In business, the staff and employees love this person. They will do anything for a P-Thinker. In business, P-Thinkers can make great leaders if they also possess the necessary business skills. When they speak, people listen.

Different Thinker, Different Entrepreneur

As you may have already guessed, each different type of thinker will be attracted to different types of entrepreneurial businesses. For example, a T-Thinker motorhead may enjoy opening an auto-parts store. An A-Thinker lawyer may like opening a law practice. A C-Thinking medical doctor may want to become a cosmetic surgeon. And P-Thinkers may become perpetual politicians, always running for office. They may also become pastors, ministering to their flock. Or they may become entertainers, getting paid to be the center of attention.

All Four Are Important

Rich dad said, "All four types of thinkers are important for a business. Small businesses stay small or fail because they lack one or more of the different types of thinkers." One of the reasons why my nylon surfer-wallet business failed was that we were too strong in the C and P categories and very weak in the A and T categories.

Many self-employed entrepreneurs are very strong in the A or T category. A person may be a great lawyer in the A category or a great electrician in the T category. These people are very smart experts in one market niche and do best on their own. They may struggle to grow because they are weak in the C or P category.

In the world of investing, an A or T person will invest differently from a C or P person. A and T people want a precise formula to follow. They want to see the numbers and analyze them repeatedly. C or P investors are more interested in exotic deals or want to know who the other players are in the deal. Notice the word player, which means people are important in the investment equation. This is important for P-Thinkers.

When I give my classes on investing, I will often have a group of people ask, "Tell me what to do. What is the formula you followed?" When I hear such questions, I know they are probably A- or T-Thinkers. It drives them crazy when I say, "We just created the investment. We got together with a group of people and put the deal together and made a lot of money." It drives them crazy because our way of investing does not fit their logic system. It is easy for A- and T-Thinkers to follow a formula such as, "Save money, get out of debt, invest for the long term, and diversify." This formula soothes their need for a logical formula for investing, even though it is not the greatest investment formula. They may get frustrated with my formulas since they may not have minds that allow flexible logic.

Rich Dad's Advice

Rich dad was concerned about my becoming an entrepreneur because I was weak in all four categories. I was not strong as an A-, T-, P-, or C-Thinker. He said, "You have to find one category and become good at it."

On a legal tablet, he wrote down the five elements of the B-I Triangle™:

1. Product

2. Legal

3. Systems

4. Communications

5. Cash flow

He then said, "I don't think you have a realistic chance in the legal, systems, or cash-flow levels of the B-I Triangle. You have not done well in school and you probably never will. I don't think you'll ever go back to school and become a lawyer, accountant, or engineer. That leaves the product level and the communications level. Choose one and commit the rest of your life to being the best at that level." And that is how I decided to leave the Marine Corps and work for the Xerox Corporation. In 1974, I decided my best chance for success as an entrepreneur was to be an expert at communicating to people. I was not a natural P-Thinker, but I decided it was a category I was willing to study for the rest of my life.

Today, I have tremendous respect for people with school smarts—people who are creative and can design products, or legal minds who have made the study of law their life, or engineers who are great at systems. I have tremendous respect for smart accountants who know how to keep track of where the cash has been flowing.

Become an Expert at Only One Level

When I asked my rich dad why I should become an expert at one level, his reply was, "If you want to have the best team around you, you need to be the best at something as well. If you are only mediocre at communications, then you will never need the best attorneys, engineers, designers, or accountants. You will only need mediocre ones because you are mediocre."

Build a Team of Experts

Some self-employed people do not do as well as they could because they feel they have to be experts at all five levels. They are often smart and good at all five levels, but they may not be strong at all levels. This may be why they often stay in the S quadrant. If you want to be a success in the B quadrant, you need to be the best at one of the levels, and then build a team of experts around you that fill in the rest of the levels.

As I overcame my shyness, I would say I became pretty good at sales, marketing, writing, speaking, and creating informational products. If not for years of training at the communication level and developing my P-Thinking abilities, I doubt if The Rich Dad Company would have become as successful as it has become.

Today, The Rich Dad Company has strong product-design teams, aggressive and smart legal teams, and established international distribution systems. It also has marketing communication systems throughout the world and a world-class accounting team that keeps the cash flowing. As a business, we have thousands of people throughout the world working for us or our products. As the old saying goes, "The Rich Dad Company was an overnight success," but it took years to get there.

Develop Yourself

The Business School of the Streets is a very tough school. I still have memories of walking around New York City, running out of money, knocking on doors, hoping to find someone who would say yes to my nylon wallets. I love New York City, yet I always know that it can be a very cruel city if you are poor, unsuccessful, and unknown.

Although The Rich Dad Company's offices are in Arizona, the engines of the business are located in New York City and cities all over the world. It is exciting to have access to the offices of some of the most powerful companies in the world such as American Express, ABC, NBC, CBS, *Fortune, Business Week* magazine, *Forbes magazine*, the *New York Times*, *New York Post*, and CNN. It is even more exciting to do, or propose to do, business with them. Yet, as successful as we have become over the last few years, I always remember the streets of New York and how cold the city can become if one of the components of the B-I Triangle™ becomes weak.

So before quitting your job, know that your most important job is to develop yourself. If you will dedicate yourself to becoming a great entrepreneur, you will find it easier to find great people to be members of your team. If you can put together a great team, you will find it easier to be successful wherever you are. Just remember, it is very important to strive to be as smart as you can be, both in street smarts and in school smarts.

RICH DAD'S
ENTREPRENEURIAL LESSON #5
The Process
Is More Important
Than the Goal

Chapter Five
MONEY TALKS

"We were rich for six months," I said. "Money was pouring in, and then the roof caved in."

"Well, at least you were millionaires, even if it was only for six months," said rich dad, chuckling. "Many people will never know what it feels like to be rich."

"Yes, and now I'm financially ruined," I whined. "Six months of success, and years to pay it back."

"Well, at least you had a taste of the good life." Rich dad smiled, doing his best to cheer me up. "Most people will never know what it feels like to build an international business and be an international success. Most people will never know what it feels like to have money pouring in the door."

"And most people will never know what it feels like to be an international failure with money pouring out the door," I said, now beginning to laugh.

"So why are you laughing?" asked rich dad.

"I don't really know," I replied. "I guess I am laughing because, as painful as it is right now, I would not trade this experience for anything. As you said, I caught a glimpse of a different world, a world very few people will ever see, a world I would like to see again. It was all so very exciting for a while."

Rich dad leaned back in his chair. For a long period of time, he seemed to sit there silently reflecting upon his life, the battles won and battles lost. Finally he came out of his thoughts and said, "Most people dash from home to work seeking security from this world. For many, work and home are where they hide from the harsh realities of a competitive world. All they want is a steady paycheck and a place to call home away from home." Rich dad again paused and then said, "And others seek something else."

"You mean something more than just security and money?" I asked.

With a wistful look in his eye, rich dad said, "Yes. If all I wanted was a secure job, a steady paycheck, and a home away from home, I would never have become an entrepreneur."

"And what were you looking for beyond security and money?" I asked.

"A different world, a different way of living. As you know, I came from a very poor family. I wanted more than just a lot of money. I wanted more than just a big house and nice cars. I wanted a life few people ever live. I knew I faced greater chances of failing than succeeding. I knew there would be highs and lows as an entrepreneur. And like everyone else, I was concerned by the highs and lows. Yet, it was the thought of a different level of life that made the risks seem worthwhile. It was not just about making money. It was about a life's adventure." Rich dad then stopped for a long moment, thinking his private thoughts.

Finally continuing, he said, "When my life is over, I already know the highs and lows will become memories of just one great adventure, of deals won and deals lost, friends made and friends lost, and of money made and money lost. It will be memories of total strangers walking in your door just to join you on your next adventure, and walking out your door once the adventure is over. And along the way, hopefully you find that place, a place with the quality and beauty of life you knew in your heart existed, that you knew in your dreams would come true."

"And have you found your place?" I asked.

Rich dad simply nodded and smiled contentedly.

A Glimpse of Your Future

With that, there really was not much more to talk about. I knew what I had to do. I had creditors to talk to and a business to repair and rebuild. I still had many things to learn so I knew it was time to get back to work. Picking up my things, I shook rich dad's hand and headed for the door.

"One more thing," said rich dad.

Turning at the door, I asked, "What is that?"

"You know those six months when you were on top of the world?"

"Yes, I do," I replied.

"That was a glimpse of your future."

"A glimpse?" I repeated. "What do you mean? A glimpse of what future?"

"In 1974, when you decided to follow my advice rather than your dad's, you began a journey, a process. The process has a beginning and an ending. It may take years, but it does have an ending. Someday this struggle you are in will suddenly end, and a new life and new process will begin. You will win if you remain faithful to this process. During this current process, you will be given many more challenges and more lessons to learn. The process is testing you as well as teaching you. If you pass the test and learn the lesson, you get to go on to your next process. If you fail a test and quit rather than retake the test, the process spits you out. So those six months of the good life were giving you a glimpse of your future, a glimpse of the world you seek, a glimpse of a world that awaits you, a glimpse of your future and a way of saying to you, 'Keep going. You're on the right track.' It's giving you a shot of courage to face the process to come and the motivation to keep going and keep learning."

"And how do you know this?" I asked. "Did you also receive a glimpse of your future when you needed it?"

Once again, rich dad simply nodded and grinned.

A Ten-Year Process

Rich dad's lesson on the subject of process has proven to be a very important lesson in my life. Looking back, it seems that my personal processes ran in approximately ten-year cycles, with each ten-year cycle a different process. For example:

- **1974 to 1984: The Learning Process**
  This is the period of time when I was learning the real-world skills of an entrepreneur. Classroom days were over and the Business School of the Streets was doing the teaching. I was making many big mistakes simply because I had a lot to learn. During this period of time, I was practicing my entrepreneurial skills building a company that manufactured nylon wallets in the Far East and marketed them throughout the world. We also designed merchandise products for rock bands such as Duran Duran, Van Halen, Judas Priest, Pink Floyd, and Boy George. At this time, I was learning as much as I could about all the elements of the B-I Triangle™. This was the real-world business school.

- **1984 to 1994: The Earning Process**
  During this period of time, I began to make a lot of money as well as build a foundation of wealth. The lessons learned from the mistakes were paying off in money. Investing that money in real estate gave Kim and me not only a foundation of assets generating passive income, but also more experience as real estate investors. During this period, I was following my passion, which was to teach entrepreneurship and investing. Our company put on courses entitled "The Business School for Entrepreneurs" and "The Business School for Investors." At this point, I was combining my poor dad's profession, teaching, with my rich dad's lessons on business and investing. This was also my time to advance my skills on the communication level of the B-I Triangle by learning to teach in ways far different than the traditional methods of teaching. As stated in a previous chapter, I had to decide which level I wanted to become an expert at. After learning the basics of all five levels, I decided that my best chance

of developing my skills was at the communication level. By being the best I could be at this level, I would have a better chance of attracting a higher caliber of team members at the other levels.

- **1994 to 2004: The Giving-Back Process**
  After Kim and I had enough money to survive on without working, I knew it was time to give back. In selling our education business, I took time to design a business that could teach my rich dad's lessons to more people at lower prices. That was the conception of The Rich Dad Company. Instead of teaching via seminars that at times cost over $5,000 to attend, I decided to create the *CASHFLOW*® game. During this period of time, my focus shifted from making money to asking myself the question, "How can I serve more people?" Ironically, I have made more money focusing on serving more people than focusing on how to make more money. In 2004, Kim and I decided that we had taken the business to a point where we needed to bring in additional management to take it to the next level—and the business has much further to go.

The ten-year cycles were not planned. It just seemed to happen that way. It was only when I looked back over my shoulder that I recognized the ten-year pattern.

Today, I live the life I caught a glimpse of in 1978. The process kept its promise to me.

The Process Is More Important Than the Goal

Most of us have heard that it is important to set goals. Yet rich dad had a different take on goals. He said, "Goals are important, but the process of obtaining the goal is far more important than the goal." Explaining, he would say, "If you ask most people, 'Who wants to be a millionaire?' most people would raise their hand. They have a goal of becoming a millionaire, but now they need to choose the process for achieving that goal. There are many ways a person can reach their goal of becoming a millionaire."

Different Processes to Become a Millionaire

Rich dad said, "The reason the process is more important than the goal is that the process determines who you become in attaining your goals. Some different processes to become rich are:

- **You can become rich by inheriting money.**
  But most of us know if we stand to inherit money—and finding a rich person willing to adopt you may prove quite difficult.

- **You can become rich by marrying for money.**
  The problem is we all know who and what you become in the process. It is the oldest profession in the world.

- **You can become rich by being cheap.**
  The problem is, if you become rich by being cheap, at the end of the process you are still cheap—and the world hates rich cheap people. In fact, the rich cheap people of the world give rich people a bad name.

- **You can become rich by being a crook.**
  The problem is, at the end of the process, you are a rich crook with crooked friends. Honest rich people do not like crooked rich people.

- **You can become rich by being lucky.**
  There are many ways to be lucky when getting rich. You can be born with great talent, as many athletes and actors are; you can win the lottery; you can be born rich; or you can just happen to be in the right place at the right time. The problem is, if you lose the money, you have to count on luck to get the money back.

- **You can become rich by becoming a smart entrepreneur.**
  To become a rich entrepreneur, you need to become a smart entrepreneur. The reason I like this process of becoming rich is that the process requires you to become smart, and becoming smart is much more important than making money. If you lose your money, this process will teach you how to get it back and become even smarter in the process.

Money Does Not Make You Rich

Lottery prizes are often in the millions of dollars simply because there are millions of people who want to become rich by being lucky. I find it interesting that this process of getting rich is not only the riskiest of all methods with the worst odds of winning, but it is a process that does not increase your financial intelligence at all. In fact, winning the lottery often reveals how low a person's financial intelligence really is. The following are stories about people who used the process of luck to become millionaires.

Two-Time Lottery Winner... Living in a Trailer

"Winning the lottery isn't always what it's cracked up to be," says Evelyn Adams, who won the New Jersey lottery not just once, but twice, to the tune of $5.4 million. Today the money is all gone, and Adams lives in a trailer.

"I won the American dream but I lost it, too. It was a very hard fall. It's called rock bottom," says Adams.

"Everybody wanted my money. Everybody had their hand out. I never learned one simple word in the English language—*No*. I wish I had the chance to do it all over again. I'd be much smarter about it now," says Adams.

A Poor Boy Who Got Lucky

Ken Proxmire was a machinist when he won $1 million in the Michigan lottery. He moved to California and went into the car business with his brothers. Within five years, he filed for bankruptcy.

"He was just a poor boy who got lucky," explains Ken's son Rick.

Living on Food Stamps

William "Bud" Post won $16.2 million in the Pennsylvania lottery but now lives on his Social Security.

"I wish it never happened. It was a total nightmare," says Post.

A former girlfriend successfully sued him for a share of his winnings. It wasn't his only lawsuit. A brother was arrested for hiring a hit man to kill him, hoping to inherit a share of the winnings. Other siblings pestered him until he agreed to invest in a car business and a restaurant in Sarasota, Florida—two ventures that brought no money back and further strained his relationship with his siblings.

Post even spent time in jail for firing a gun over the head of a bill collector.

Within a year, he was $1 million in debt. He admits he was both foolish and careless, trying to please his family. Now he lives quietly on his monthly Social Security check and food stamps.

What If You Lost a Billion Dollars?

Years ago, a reporter asked Henry Ford, a billionaire when a billion dollars was worth much more than it is today, "What if you lost everything?" Ford's response was, "I'd have it back in less than five years." When you contrast Henry Ford's response to the responses of the lottery winners, I believe you get the difference between the process of becoming a millionaire by luck and that of becoming a billionaire by being an entrepreneur.

A Question to Think About

After reading Henry Ford's response, I often ask myself, "If I lost it all, how much would I recover in five years?" If my past is any indicator, each time I hit zero—and I did hit zero a number of times—I came roaring back making much more money than I lost. I've not made a billion dollars as Henry Ford did, but my businesses have had income in the hundreds of millions of dollars. In my opinion, the entrepreneur's process is the best process to get rich because it is also an educational process to achieving great wealth—if you have the heart, mind, and stamina for it.

Pouring the Foundation

The educational process of becoming an entrepreneur requires the entrepreneur to learn and gain experience in the five levels of the B-I Triangle™. Once a person becomes somewhat proficient in all five levels, life is pretty good.

It took me about ten years as an undergraduate student of the Business School of the Streets to attain a basic level of proficiency. Can a person attain proficiency at all five levels faster? Absolutely. One of the reasons for writing this book was to simply inform you of the levels. If you know about the levels, it makes it easier to focus your learning activities and personal development, level by level.

Why Cash Flow Is the Base Level

Most wannabe entrepreneurs focus on the product level, the top level of the B-I Triangle™. While product is important, looking at the B-I Triangle, you notice that cash flow is the base level with the most area allocated to it.

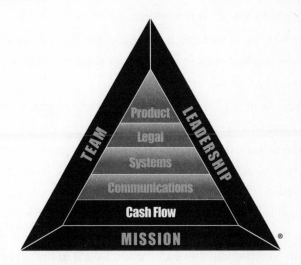

When I first started out as a professional entrepreneur, I used to get excited looking at new products or ideas. That is how I got caught up in the nylon-wallet business. The nylon wallet was just one of about 50 different product ideas we considered. Some of the other ideas were wooden puzzles, sugar packets with Hawaiian pictures on the packets wrapped in a burlap box, a magazine, and even candy bullets packaged in a box that said, "Bite the Bullet." As you can tell, our C-Thinking ability was unlimited.

As soon as we decided on the nylon wallet as our product, the three of us began designing its packaging. Again, this required C-Thinking, which all three of us enjoyed. It was not long before we were hitting the streets looking for investors. Most potential investors were polite and took time to look at our product and its packaging. Then, if they were interested, they all asked the same questions: "May I see your numbers? What are your projections?" When we did not have the answers, we were turned down and turned down quickly.

Even rich dad turned us down, but he did not turn us down politely. He was furious. Kicking my two partners out of his office, he closed the door behind them and gave me one of the most severe reprimands I have ever had from either of my dads. I have written about this incident in other books, so I will not retell the details of the story, yet the lesson is worth repeating. The lesson is, for successful business people and investors, the numbers are very important.

Today, older, wiser, and much wealthier, whenever I am asked to evaluate a new product or business, I do the same thing those investors did to me years ago—I ask for the numbers.

This does not mean I am any better at reading or producing numbers today than I was in 1978. The difference is, I ask for them and then ask someone who is trained at reading the numbers to go over the numbers with me. My level of expertise is the communications level, and I do go over that portion of the business plan carefully. I am pretty good at the communications level but not that good at the cash-flow level. But that is not an excuse for me to ignore the cash-flow level, or any level for that matter. As an entrepreneur and an investor, I need to know the entire business, not just the parts of the business I am interested in.

If a wannabe entrepreneur asks to show me a new product, the first question I ask is: "Do you have financial projections?" Or if the business is an established business, I will ask: "Do you have financial statements?" Again, I ask these questions not because I am great at numbers, but as a test of the wannabe entrepreneur's knowledge of what it takes to be an entrepreneur.

If the wannabe entrepreneur does have actual numbers or projections, I will ask someone else whose strength is in accounting to come with me to interpret the numbers. The numbers tell a story, and I need someone who can read the numbers and interpret them to tell me the story. As an entrepreneur, I believe it is very important to tell your business story in numbers.

It's Better to Pay Early

If you are serious about becoming an entrepreneur, an interesting exercise is to hire an experienced accountant to help you with a proposed budget and cash-flow analysis. Even if you do not go through with the product or the business, the exercise will give you a better idea of what it costs to start and run a business. Once you know your budget, you will have an idea of how much you will have to sell to support the business. The experienced accountant may also point out expenses you may not know about. I wish I had done this exercise before starting my nylon surfer-wallet business. I might not have lost as much money as I did. The cost of hiring a trained accountant for guidance would have been a drop in the bucket compared to the money I lost. More important, the money you spend for an accountant will be priceless in your educational development as an entrepreneur.

If you ask most accountants, I am certain they will tell you that most entrepreneurs lack knowledge of accounting laws and practices and are horrible at recordkeeping. Their lack of accuracy with numbers may eventually get them in trouble. It is this lack of knowledge that eventually costs them even more money. In other words, pay them a little early rather than pay a lot more later.

Why I Created the Board Game

One of the primary reasons I created the *CASHFLOW*® board game is the reprimand my rich dad gave me back in the 1970s. For most of my life, rich dad had been emphasizing the importance of the numbers, and I sincerely thought I understood them. It was not until he chewed me out when I lost so much money that I began to understand why he put such emphasis on the numbers. Today I understand.

The game serves as a communication bridge between you and your accountant. It will not make you an accountant. The game will give you the advantage of being more familiar with the T-Thinking and A-Thinking logic of the accounting profession.

If you are like me, weak at the subject of accounting and numbers, I strongly suggest you use the *CASHFLOW*® games as an educational tool.

Again, before quitting your job to start your business, I recommend that you sit down with an experienced accountant and go over a budget on what it may cost to start and operate your business. If the numbers shock you, simply take a deep breath and sleep on it for a night or two. Give yourself time to expand your mind around the costs. The cost of starting, building, or growing a business is often more than originally imagined.

Keep Your Job

If the costs frighten you off, then maybe being an entrepreneur is not for you. High expenses are an everyday challenge in business. Taking on that challenge is one of the most important jobs of an entrepreneur. It requires a lot of A-, T-, P-, and C-Thinking power to solve these challenges. Personally, I do not like the challenges, but every time I have taken them on, I have become a better, wiser, and more confident entrepreneur.

Show Me the Numbers

When wannabe entrepreneurs call looking for money, they fall into two categories.

1. Those with a business plan and financial projections

2. Those with nothing

If a person comes with empty hands, it either means they are very early in the process, or they don't have a clue what they are doing, or both. Talking only about the product without financial projections indicates these people have not really thought through the process. If I am interested, I may suggest they go back to the drawing board, follow the B-I Triangle™ as an outline, and then hire an accountant and come up with a business plan, which includes a set of numbers.

One Step to Raising Money

Whenever someone asks, "How do I raise money for my business?" I respond by asking, "Do you have a business plan?" A good business plan with a great presentation can raise the money you need. A bad business plan with a poor presentation can lose you money.

This does not mean that the numbers of the business plan are cast in stone. The financial results of most start-up businesses do not typically follow the plan or precisely meet the projections. The process of creating a business plan with numbers is an A-Thinking and T-Thinking process that causes the entrepreneur to think through the venture in more detail and then put it down on paper. Remember that a successful business is created before there is a business.

The plan does not have to be elaborate. It can be very simple. A plan simply lets the potential investor see the thoughts inside the mind of the entrepreneur. Also, it allows the investor to know that the person is serious about the proposed business.

Again, even if the business does not take shape, the process of thinking through the creation of a business, putting it down on paper, and matching it with numbers that tell the same story is an excellent educational process and reality check. It begins to balance school smarts and street smarts.

Tell Me a Story

A number of years ago, a young man called me and asked for an appointment. When I asked for what purpose, he said, "I have a business proposal I would like to present to you."

"Are you looking for investment money?" I asked directly.

He stumbled and haltingly said, "Yes. I am."

Normally I do not look at businesses at this early stage, yet I was curious and agreed to meet him for lunch.

A week later, I met him at a local restaurant. He was well dressed and had an impressive-looking business plan. As I said, I am not good at reading the numbers, yet I do my best to listen to the story the numbers and the plan are telling me. The first thing I look at is the salary-and-wages line of the financial projections. For me, that is where the story begins.

This young man had himself down for a $120,000-a-year salary. My first question was, "Why do you need such a high salary from a business that does not exist?"

"Well, that is what I am being paid at my job today," he replied, a little indignantly. "Besides, I have a wife and three kids in school. It's the bare minimum I can live on."

"Okay," I said and continued looking at the business plan. As I said, the business plan and the financial projections tell a story. The salary-requirement line was introducing me to the lead character, the hero of the story. I was gaining a glimpse into his brain, how he thought, how he spent money, and the priorities of his personal life.

Seeing his salary requirements and getting into his head, I felt he was still thinking like an employee, looking for a high-paying job. As far as I was concerned, the lunch was over. I had seen enough just by getting to know the hero of the story. I knew that I did not want to invest in his business.

Relating the Financial Statement to the B-I Triangle™

Since we had not yet ordered lunch, and I still had to be polite, I looked next at the other expenses of the business and how they related to the B-I Triangle. In other words, my first step was to call on my P-Thinking mind. I needed to get a sense of who this person was in front of me. My second step was to call on the C-Thinking, A-Thinking, and T-Thinking minds and create a relationship between the financial statement and the five levels of the B-I Triangle.

The diagram in my mind looked like this.

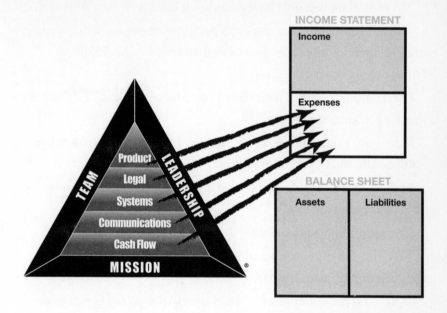

My next question was, "What do you do for your current employer? What is your job?"

"I am a mechanical engineer by training," he replied. "I work in customer service—tracking customer orders through our system. That is where I developed my product. Let me tell you about it."

"Just a moment," I said. "I just have a few questions about your projections." Pointing at the line entitled "Advertising and Promotion," I asked, "What is this expense for $10,000 a month? What is your marketing plan?"

"Oh, I haven't given that much thought yet. My plan is to hire an agency and let them handle our marketing."

"Have you had much experience in sales or marketing?" I asked.

"No, I haven't," he said. "I've spent most of my career working on the internal systems of a business. That is where I got my idea for my new product. It will revolutionize order tracking."

"Have you talked to an intellectual-property attorney to protect your idea?"

"Well, I have looked, but I really have not found one yet."

"In your plan, you only have $4,000 for attorneys' fees. Why is that?"

"Well, I wanted to keep my expenses down. Later on, when money comes in, then I'll hire more attorneys. For now, I think $4,000 is adequate to get me off the ground."

"And who helped you with these projections?" I asked. "I do not see a line for accounting expenses."

"Oh, you're right. I forgot that expense. How much do you think should be allocated to accounting fees?"

"I don't know," I said. "I'm not an accountant. If you really want to know, you should ask one."

"How do I find a good one?"

"You can call my accountant, but he is very expensive and may be more than you need at this stage."

"Oh," said the entrepreneur. "I am trying to keep my expenses down. I'll look for a cheaper accountant."

Lack of Real-World Experience

Although this was hardly an in-depth look at the business, I had heard enough of the story. Eventually I did get a look at his product, which never should have happened if he had had an intellectual-property attorney's advice. He did not have me sign any document saying I would keep the product a secret—a big and clear indicator of this wannabe entrepreneur's lack of real-world experience.

My Own Lesson Learned

If I had liked the product, I could have simply taken his idea and taken it to market. How do I know this? Painfully, I know this lesson because I made the same mistake he was making. In 1977, I should have patented my nylon shoe-pocket wallet for runners, but I decided to save a few dollars by not hiring a patent attorney.

That is why, after coming up with the idea for the *CASHFLOW*® board game, I did not tell anyone about the game except for Kim and my engineer behind the game. The first person I went to find was an intellectual-property attorney.

This is one more example of turning bad luck into good luck. Because of my inexperience and my desire to save a few dollars by not patenting my nylon wallet, I subsequently lost millions of dollars. That bad luck was turned into good luck when I learned from that mistake by patenting my *CASHFLOW®* board game.

One reason why the legal level lies just below the product level of the B-I Triangle™ is that the entrepreneur's ideas are often the company's most important assets. The attorney's job is to protect the company, its products, and its intellectual property—*before* there is a product or a business. You need protect your ideas, your most important asset.

Saying No

The young engineer looked good. He had the look of a successful business leader. His new product looked promising. Yet I said, "No, I don't think I will invest in your business." The cash-flow level of the B-I Triangle had revealed his strengths and weaknesses as an entrepreneur. In the end, I was not saying no to his product or ideas. I was saying no to him. He still had a lot of homework to do.

Although the product looked promising, the entrepreneur's story did not. He might succeed, but I had my doubts. If he did succeed, I doubted if he had the ability to grow the business to a point where, as an investor, I could get my money back. So I passed on the opportunity to invest with him.

There Are No Bad Investments

My rich dad often said, "There are no bad investments, but there are many bad investors." He also said, "There are no bad business opportunities, but there are many bad entrepreneurs." In my opinion, this young engineer had a great idea for a great new product. However, his ideas about business were not so great.

What rich dad wanted to pound into our heads was that the world was filled with mega-million-dollar opportunities. The problem is that there are more mega-million-dollar opportunities than there are mega-million-dollar entrepreneurs. That is why the cash-flow level of the B-I Triangle™ is so important. It tells the story, not of the opportunity, but of the entrepreneur. This is especially true in the creation phase of the business, when the business is not yet a business.

Red Flags

One reason why your banker does not ask you for your school report card or your grade point average or what subject you majored in, is that a banker is not looking for a measure of your academic intelligence. Your banker is looking for your level of financial intelligence, which indicates your level of financial responsibility—how much you earn, what you spend your money on, and how much you keep. When looking at financial projections, or better yet, the actual financial numbers from an existing business, I have learned to look for similar indicators. When looking at the numbers, forecast or actual, there are certain items that are red flags for me.

Red flag #1: Extravagant salaries

You may have already noticed that I looked at that line first. It tells me a lot about the entrepreneur. One thing it tells me is what is more important to the entrepreneurs—the business or their personal lives. Many, many times, I have met entrepreneurs who rape, starve, and torture their business rather than feed and nurture the business. A friend of mine consulted with a building-maintenance company in Denver that was having cash-flow problems. The business had great contracts with offices and apartment houses to keep the parking areas swept in summer and free of snow in winter. With low overhead and high margins, the company should have been doing well. Instead, the business was always in financial trouble.

Upon further inspection, my friend found that the owner had expensive ski chalets in Vail and Aspen with the accoutrements (doodads) to match. On top of that, the company had flashy cars and threw lavish parties, all at company expense. To make matters even worse, he had been lying to the IRS and the state tax department, and his actions were starting to border on tax evasion rather than tax avoidance.

When my friend recommended that he sell his houses and his cars, cut back on his spending, and hire a high-powered accounting firm to beg for mercy, my friend was fired. The owner still thought there was something wrong with the business. This is an extreme example of an entrepreneur putting his needs before the needs of the business. The numbers of the business told the story of both the business and the entrepreneur.

Red flag #2: Good expenses and bad expenses

This is one of rich dad's most important lessons. He said, "The reason so many people are poor is that they are poor spenders. In other words, there are good expenses and bad expenses." He also said, "The rich are rich because they have expenses that make them rich. The poor are poor because they have expenses that make them poor." Regarding the subject of entrepreneurship, he said, "Most people are not good entrepreneurs because they are savers rather than smart spenders."

One of the downfalls of my nylon surfer-wallet business was my desire to save money and not spend $7,000 on patent-attorney fees. Saving a few thousand dollars cost me a multimillion-dollar business. My lesson was to learn to spend money that made me money.

A friend of a friend has always had a tough time in her business. Over lunch with her, she told me she was spending $50,000 redecorating her apartment. When I asked her if she owned the apartment, she said, "No. I don't have enough money for a down payment so I just rent." When I quizzed her as to why she would spend so much money on a property she didn't own, she got angry. "Well, I need to have a nice place to live." At that moment, I believe I got a glimpse of what caused her business struggles. She simply spends money foolishly.

One of the reasons the B-I Triangle™ is named after the B and I quadrants on the right side of the CASHFLOW Quadrant® is that an individual must know how to spend money and get that money back with a respectable return on the right side of the Quadrant. One of the reasons people on the E and S side of the Quadrant have a tough time as entrepreneurs is simply that they know how to work for money, but they do not know how to spend money and then have the money come back with more money. This ability to spend money and have your money come back with more money is essential to entrepreneurs and investors on the B and I side of the CASHFLOW Quadrant.

Between 1997 and 2005, the real estate market boomed. Even though the market boomed, I met many individuals who invested in real estate and failed to make any money. To me, this is a signal that this person does not know how to spend money and have the money return with more money. These people may not make good entrepreneurs or they need to work on their business skills. When I look at the numbers of a business, I am looking for this ability to spend money and have the money return with more money. This is an essential skill.

Red flag #3: Money talks
Rich dad said, "There is a big difference between a business and busyness. The reason most people do not make good entrepreneurs is that they are busy and work hard, but they do not make any money. An entrepreneur must make money. That money shows up at the cash-flow level of the B-I Triangle.

A few years ago, I read an article about a couple who were both laid off. Both were highly paid marketing executives with a major New York firm, making over $250,000 combined income. After a year in their own business as marketing experts, their business earned less than $26,000. Why? I suspect one reason was that, as high-paid corporate employees, they were never held accountable to the bottom line of the company they worked for. As entrepreneurs, owners of their own business, they had to be very accountable. They found out that their marketing skills in the corporate world did not translate to financial success on the streets.

Suddenly they found out that owning a business does not mean simply working hard and being busy. Owning a business means your activities show up directly on the bottom line as money made and money lost. Rich dad would say, "An employee can be paid for being busy. An entrepreneur is paid for results." The results are often known as the bottom line. That is why the cash-flow level is the base of the B-I Triangle™. As rich dad said, "You do not need a safe-deposit box for excuses."

To me, certain red flags indicate the entrepreneur is stuck in a part of the developmental process. Will the entrepreneur learn from the process and move on, or keep raising the same red flags?

Red flags occur in life as well as in business. Whenever someone gets stuck in their process, I have noticed that life sends up red flags of its own. They can be warnings such as bad health, bad luck, or bad relationships. Rich dad said, "Red flags are warnings. We can choose to heed the warning and learn, or ignore the warning. If you do not heed the warning, the process may change directions on you and a new process may begin."

My real dad smoked two to three packs of cigarettes a day. The red flags were flying for most of his life. He did not heed the warnings and was eventually diagnosed with lung cancer. He finally quit smoking, but it was too late. One process ended, and a new one began. His next process was a battle for life, a battle he lost a year later.

Be Accountable

There is an overused statement that goes, "Money talks and BS walks." Where money talks the loudest is on the bottom line of a financial statement. As an entrepreneur, you do not have to be an accountant, but you do need to be accountable.

Before you quit your job, please remember two things:

1. Employees and advisors are not responsible for the bottom line. Entrepreneurs are.

2. When you look at the CASHFLOW Quadrant®,

people on the E and S side of the Quadrant are not required to have financial statements. However, financial statements are required by people on the B and I side. Why? Because money talks and the story it tells is of the financial acumen of the individual in the B or I quadrant. These individuals are measured by their financial successes in the B or I quadrant.

Think Like a CFO

If you would like to improve your financial skills at the cashflow level of the B-I Triangle™, I strongly recommend you get the *CASHFLOW*® game and play it often. The game teaches you to think like a CFO, a chief financial officer, an important member of any entrepreneurial team.

The Buck Stops with the Entrepreneur

A CEO or entrepreneur cannot pass the buck. Making excuses or blaming subordinates is never attractive. The buck stops with the entrepreneur or CEO. That is why the cash-flow level is the base level of the B-I Triangle. That is where the bucks stop. As an entrepreneur, you are the person responsible for the entire B-I Triangle. So before you quit your job, always remember where the buck stops, and that money talks.

RICH DAD'S
ENTREPRENEURIAL LESSON #6

The Best Answers Are Found in Your Heart, Not in Your Head

THE THREE KINDS OF MONEY

What did you learn in Vietnam?" asked rich dad.

"I learned the importance of mission, leadership, and the team," I replied.

"Which was the most important?"

"The mission."

"Good." Rich dad smiled. "You'll make a good entrepreneur."

A Green Marine

In early 1972, my job was to pilot a UH-1 Huey helicopter gunship in Vietnam. After two months in the war zone, my copilot and I had flown several missions but had not yet encountered enemy fire. This was soon to change. On the day I finally met the enemy, things were already very tense for me. We flew with our doors open, and the wind chattered through the aircraft. Looking back at the aircraft carrier, our home, I was once again reminded that this was a war zone and my school days were over. For two years I had trained for this mission.

I knew that each time we crossed the beach and flew over land, there were real live enemy soldiers with real guns and real bullets waiting for us. Turning to look back at my crew of three, two machine gunners and a crew chief, I asked on the intercom, "Are you guys ready?" Not saying anything, they simply gave me a thumbs-up.

My crew knew I was green and untested. They knew I could fly, but they did not know how I would perform under the pressure of combat.

Initially there were two helicopters in our flight. About twenty minutes into the flight, the lead aircraft had to turn back. Apparently there were electrical problems. We were told by the powers-that-be on the aircraft carrier to continue and to remain on call in the area. You could feel the tension mount in our aircraft because the lead aircraft had the more experienced pilots. They had been in combat for over eight months. On top of that, their aircraft carried air-to-ground rockets. My aircraft only had machine guns. As the lead aircraft turned and headed back toward the ship, the anxiety in my aircraft was very real. None of us liked being out there alone.

We passed over some of the most beautiful beaches in the world and headed north. We had dark green rice paddies to our left, blue-green ocean to our right, and white sand beaches below us. Suddenly over the radio, two Army helicopters broadcast that they needed help. They were in a battle with a fifty-caliber machine gun in the hills beyond the rice paddies. Being close by, we responded and began flying toward their location. Flying just below the clouds, we soon saw the Army helicopters in a firefight with the machine gun on the ground. There was also a lot of small-arms fire coming from enemy troops in the area. It was easy to tell the difference between the rounds from the thirty-caliber guns that the troops carried and the heavier fifty-caliber rounds from the machine gun. The tracers from the thirty-caliber small-arms fire looked like hot red-orange specks zipping up against the dark green sky. The fifty-caliber tracer rounds looked like flying ketchup bottles. I took a very deep breath and kept flying.

Watching the battle as we flew closer, I kept hoping the Army helicopters would destroy the machine gun and not need our help. But no luck. When one of the Army helicopters was hit and fell from the sky, I knew we were going to be part of the fight. As the smoking helicopter spiraled to the ground, the tension climbed even more in our aircraft. Looking back at my crew, I simply said, "Clear the decks. Make the guns hot. We're going in." I did not know what we were going to do. I simply knew we had to be prepared for the worst.

The second Army helicopter broke off from the fight and went down to pick up the crew of the first helicopter. That left us—a single aircraft with only thirty-caliber machine guns, about to face an estimated 15 troops with guns and a fifty-caliber machine gun. I wanted to turn and run. I knew that it was the smart thing to do. Yet, not wanting to appear like a wimp to my men, I kept flying toward the location of the fifty-caliber machine gun. I was now flying on pure bravado and hoping for the best.

With the two Army helicopters out of the way, the ground fire turned on us. Although it was far away, seeing real live rounds being fired at me was a sight and feeling I will never forget.

My crew had been in this situation before. Their silence told me that this was a particularly bad situation to be in. As the first fifty-caliber rounds came up short of our aircraft, my crew chief tapped me on the helmet, pulled and turned my helmet so we were face to face and said, "Hey, Lieutenant, do you know what is bad about this job?"

Shaking my head, I feebly said, "No."

Smiling his broad toothy grin, the crew chief, on his second tour in Vietnam, said, "The problem with this job is there is no second best. If you decide to fight, either we are going home today or those guys on the ground are going home. But both of us aren't going home. One of us is about to die. It's up to you to decide which one of us that is—them or us."

Looking back at my gunners, young men of 19 and 20, I spoke into the intercom again and said, "You guys ready?" Both young men gave me a thumbs-up, as all good Marines are trained to do. They were ready. They were trained to follow orders, regardless of whether their leader was competent or not. Realizing their lives were in my hands did not make me feel any better. At that moment, I stopped thinking only about myself and began thinking about all of us.

Silently I shouted to myself, "Think. Should we turn and run, or should we fight?" Then my mind began feeding me excuses as to why we should turn and run. "You're a single aircraft. There should be at least two aircraft. Isn't there a rule saying you cannot fight unless there are two aircraft? The lead pilots are gone. They had the rockets. No one will blame us if we turn and run. Maybe we can go down and help the Army pilots. Yeah, let's go help them. Then we don't have to do our job. Then we have an excuse for not fighting. We were on a rescue mission. We saved some Army fliers. Yeah, that sounds good."

Then I asked myself, "What if we miraculously win? What if we beat that fifty-cal and live? What will we get?"

The answer came back, "We all might receive some medal for bravery. We'll be heroes."

"And what if we lose?"

The answer came back, "We'll be dead or captured."

Glancing back at the two young gunners, I decided their lives were worth more than a medal on a ribbon. So was mine, I admitted to myself. Being brave and stupid was ruled out.

The fifty-caliber rounds were flying closer to us. The gunner on the ground was increasing his accuracy with every shot. Back at flight school, we learned that a fifty-caliber round had a greater range than a thirty-caliber round. We had thirty-caliber machine guns. That meant he was going to be able to hit us long before we could get to him. Suddenly, a burst of fifty-caliber rounds zoomed just past my window. Without thinking, I banked to the left and dove toward the ground to increase the distance between the enemy gunner and us. Since I had no idea what I was doing, I decided it was time to think. Flying straight into the machine gunner was certain death. As my aircraft was diving toward the ground in a sharp left bank, I used my radio and broadcast to anyone in the area, "This is Marine helicopter, Yankee-Tango-96, fifty-cal located. Need help."

Out of the blue, a loud clear confident voice crackled through my headset, "Yankee-Tango 96, flight of four Marine A-4s RTB (returning to base) have extra ordinance and fuel on board. Give us your position, and we'll give you a hand."

Relief ran through our crew as I radioed our position to the Marine Corps pilots of the jets. In a few minutes, I could see four specks flying low to the ground coming to our assistance. Seeing us, the flight leader radioed, "Before we get too close, fly back toward Charlie and see if you can draw his fire. Once we see his tracers, we'll take care of the rest." With that, we turned and once again flew toward the fifty-caliber machine gun. Once his tracers began flying at us again, the wing leader of the four jets radioed, "Target in sight." In less than five minutes, the fifty-caliber machine gun was no longer a problem. My crew and I were the ones who went home that night.

Different Teams, Same Mission

There have been many times I sit quietly and reflect on that day. Although I said, "Thank you," over the air, once the fight was over, I still wish I had had the chance to meet those guys in person, shake their hands and say, "Thank you." We were on different teams from different ships, but we all shared the same mission.

All wars are horrible. War is simply humanity at its worst. War is a time when we use our best technology and our bravest people to kill our fellow human beings. During my year in Vietnam, I saw the worst of humanity. I saw sights I wish I had never seen. I also caught glimpses of a spiritual power, a dedication to a higher calling, I would never have witnessed if I had not gone to war. When the term *band of brothers* is used to describe the bond between soldiers, I wonder if someone who has never fought in a war can ever know what that bond feels like. For me, it is a spiritual bond dedicated to a higher calling—something known as a mission.

Mission Statements

In business today, it is very fashionable to tout one's mission statement, the sole driving purpose for forming the business. After my Marine Corps and Vietnam experience, I have remained skeptical each time someone says, "The mission of our business is..." My skepticism causes me to wonder how much the word *mission* is just that—only a word.

The Stronger Mission Wins

One day, I was flying near the DMZ, the Demilitarized Zone that used to separate North Vietnam from South Vietnam. Looking down upon the carnage raging below me, I noticed something that deeply disturbed me. Returning to the aircraft carrier that night, I raised my hand during the debriefing and asked, "Why do their Vietnamese fight harder than our Vietnamese? Are we fighting for the wrong side? Are we fighting for the wrong cause?"

Needless to say, I was threatened with a court-martial for such treasonous-sounding words. To me, I was not being treasonous. I was only asking a question. I was simply expressing an observation, something I had noticed since arriving in Vietnam. It seemed to me that the Viet Cong and the North Vietnamese soldiers fought harder, tougher, and with more tenacity than our Vietnamese soldiers. From my perspective, the Vietnamese soldiers on our side did not seem to fight as hard. Personally, I did not feel we could count on them. I often wondered if we stopped paying them, would they keep fighting?

To be fair, there were many U.S. soldiers who were not there to fight either. Many were draftees who were unlucky enough to be drafted. If they were offered a choice of a plane ticket home or to stay and fight, many would have been on the plane.

Halfway through my tour, I realized we were not going to win. We were not going to win, even though we were better equipped, had the best technology, overwhelming firepower, the highest pay, and well-trained men and women. I knew we were not going to win simply because our side, the South Vietnamese as well as the Americans, lacked a strong enough mission, a higher calling, a reason to fight. We had lost our hearts. At least, I had lost mine. I did not want to kill anymore. I was no longer a good Marine.

My experience in Vietnam proved to me that the stronger mission wins. The same thing happens in business.

A Vow of Poverty

Most of us know that men and women of religious faith have taken vows of poverty in support of their spiritual mission. When I was a little boy, my dad explained to me that his friend, a Catholic priest, had taken a vow of poverty. Asking him what that meant, he said, "He has dedicated his life to God and God's work. That means money is not to be a part of his life. He lives an austere life in the service of God."

"What does *austere* mean?" I asked.

Tiring of the thousand questions a child asks, my dad's answer was, "Never mind what *austere* means. You'll find out later on."

A number of years later, I found out what *austere* meant. Sitting in a classroom for new Marine Corps officers, the instructor explained to the class that throughout history, men and women of war have also taken vows of poverty. The instructor said, "In the feudal times, many knights took a vow of poverty in order to be true to their calling. They did not want money or desire worldly goods to interfere with their dedication to God and king."

Before joining the Marine Corps, I was a ship's officer on an oil tanker for Standard Oil of California. I was being paid over $4,000 a month, which was a lot of money in 1969. Even though I was draft-exempt because I was sailing for the oil industry, a classification known as nondefense vital industry, both my dads encouraged me to serve my country in time of war. As a Marine Corps officer, my pay dropped to less than $300 a month. Sitting in that classroom, listening to the instructor remind us that throughout history, men and women of war took vows of poverty, I finally found my definition of the word *austere*, the definition my dad did not give me some years before.

Three Kinds of Income, Three Kinds of Money

There are three kinds of income.

1. Ordinary income
2. Portfolio income
3. Passive income

My poor dad worked for ordinary income, the highest-taxed income there is. My rich dad worked primarily for passive income, the lowest-taxed income. These terms for the three types of income actually come from the Internal Revenue Service. The tax department taxes the three incomes at different rates. An entrepreneur has the opportunity to work for all three types of income and needs to know the differences because the different tax rates can make a huge difference to the bottom line. I mention these incomes now not to confuse you, but to distinguish them from the discussion on the three different types of money I am about to discuss.

While we were in high school, rich dad taught his son and me that people work for three different types of money. They are:

1. Competitive money

2. Cooperative money

3. Spiritual money

Competitive Money

To explain competitive money, he said, "We learn to compete early in life. We compete in school for grades, we compete in sports, and we compete for the person we love. At work, we learn to compete for jobs, for raises, for promotions, for recognition, and for survival. In business, companies compete for customers, market share, contracts, and good employees. Competition is survival of the fittest, "dog eat dog." Most people work for competitive money."

Cooperative Money

To explain cooperative money, he said, "In sports and in business, cooperation is known as teamwork. The richest, most powerful entrepreneurs have built the biggest businesses in the world via cooperation. They become more competitive due to the cooperation of their team. Most entrepreneurs of large businesses are great team leaders."

Spiritual Money

Explaining spiritual money was a little bit more difficult. He said, "Spiritual money is created by doing God's work—work that God wants done. It's work being done in response to a higher calling."

Not understanding what rich dad meant, I asked him, "You mean like forming a church?"

His reply was, "There are entrepreneurs who do form churches, just as there are entrepreneurs who form charities. Both could be examples of working for spiritual money, but spiritual money is not restricted to simply a church or charity."

For years, this category puzzled me, and I often had discussions with him on this subject. During one of these discussions he said, "Most people go to work for money—nothing else. They do not care if it is competitive, cooperative, or spiritual. For many people, work and money are just a means to an end. If you paid them twice as much to not work, many would take your offer."

"You mean they would not work for free?" I asked with a smirk.

"No, definitely not. If you did not pay most people, they would move on looking for another job. They may want to help you and your business, but they have bills to pay and families to feed. They need money, any kind of money. They would choose their job depending upon which one paid the most and had the best benefits."

"So is spiritual money like loving your work and doing what you love?"

"No," smiled rich dad. "Doing what you love is not what I mean by spiritual money."

"So what is spiritual money?" I asked. "Is it working for free?"

"No, that is not it either. It's not about working for free because spiritual money is not really about money."

"Spiritual money is not about money? If it is not about money, then what is it about?" I asked.

"It's about doing a job not because you want to do it, but because it must be done and you know deep down in your soul, you're the one that is supposed to do it."

"How do you know you're supposed to do it?" I asked.

"Because it disturbs you that no one else is doing it. You may say to yourself, 'Why isn't someone doing something about this?'"

"Could it anger you?" I asked.

"Oh, yes," said rich dad softly. "It can also sadden you or even break your heart. It may seem like an injustice or a crime to you. It probably disturbs your sense of decency. It seems unfair—an injustice."

"Don't most people have these feelings about something in their life?" I asked.

"Yes, but most people don't do anything about it. They go to work and say things such as, 'Why doesn't the government do something about it?' or they write letters to the editor and complain."

"But they don't do anything about it," I added.

Quietly, rich dad said, "In most cases, no. They may talk about it, they may complain about it, but they do little about it. After all, they are too busy at their job, earning enough money to pay the rent and saving enough money to take the kids to Disneyland."

"What would happen if they did do something about it?" I asked. "What might happen?"

"If they were truly committed to solving the problem, I would say that the invisible forces of this universe, of God, might come to their support. Magic might happen in their lives. This is when spiritual money comes into play. But it is more than money. People you never met before come to join forces with you—not for the money, but for the mission."

"Why do they join you?" I asked.

"Because they are on the same mission."

That was about all I could handle that day. I had a test the next day and my mission at the time was to get out of high school.

Giving Your Gift

About a year went by and once again I brought up the subject of spiritual money. "If I simply work on a problem I know needs to be worked on, will that bring in the invisible forces, the spiritual money?"

Rich dad laughed and said, "Maybe and maybe not. I'm not the one who makes those decisions. I will say this. One of the keys to attracting the invisible magical forces is to be dedicated to giving your gift."

"What?" I responded with a jolt. "Giving my gift? What do you mean by a gift?"

"A special God-given talent," rich dad replied. "Something you are the best at. A talent God gave especially to you."

"And what would that be?" I asked. "There is nothing I know of that I am the best at."

"Well, you have to find it."

"Does everybody have one?"

"I'd like to think so," smiled rich dad.

"If everyone has a gift, why are so many people below average?" I asked.

Rich dad roared with laughter at that question. Finally composing himself, he said, "Because finding your gift, developing your gift, and giving your gift is very hard work. Most people do not want to work that hard."

Now I was puzzled. It seemed to me that if God had given us a gift, it should be apparent. It should be easily accessible. When I asked rich dad to clarify this, he said, "Great doctors spend years in school and then practice for years developing their gift. Great golfers have practiced for years developing their gift. While there are the exceptions such as child prodigies, most people have to dedicate their life to finding and developing their gift. Unfortunately, the world is filled with gifted people who never develop their gift. Finding one's gift can be hard work, and then developing one's gift can be even harder work. And that is why so many people appear to be below average."

"So that is why most professional athletes practice harder than amateurs?" I asked. "They dedicate their life to developing their strength and skills in order to develop their gift."

Rich dad nodded.

Once again, I had heard more than I could handle. The discussion was over, but I remembered the lesson.

Good Is the Enemy of Great

There are two books I recommend to friends who are dedicated to becoming the best they can be in life. I strongly recommend both books for anyone dedicated to becoming a great entrepreneur. The first one is *Good to Great* by Jim Collins. We have read and held study groups on this book five times. Each time our group studied the book in depth, it seemed like we were reading a different book.

The opening line of *Good to Great* says it all. Collins begins by stating, "Good is the enemy of great." Keeping with the subject of finding one's gift, we all know the world is filled with good business people, good athletes, good parents, good workers, and good governments. But the world has a shortage of great business people, great athletes, great parents, great workers, great governments, and so on. Why? Because for many of us, good is good enough. If my rich dad were here today, he would say, "Bringing out your gift is about bringing out your greatness, not just what you are good enough at."

Good to Great is filled with lessons essential for big and small businesses. In our study groups, each person seemed to find a lesson that was written just for him or her. For me, the lesson that hit me the hardest was the lesson that greatness is a choice. It is not about being gifted or talented or more fortunate than others. It's about a choice we all can make.

Being a person who has been average and below average for most of my life, the idea that I had the choice to change all that was a message from the book that went straight to my heart and my soul.

Overcome Your Resistance

The War of Art by Steven Pressfield is another book for anyone who wants to make the best of their lives. *The War of Art* is about the self-saboteur in all of us. Steven Pressfield identifies resistance as that force inside each of us that holds us back. I know this character named resistance well. Except in my case, my resistance comes in different characters with different names. In the morning, my resistance goes by the name of Fat Boy. As I awake, look at my clock, and say, "Time to go to the gym," immediately Fat Boy says, "Oh, no, not this morning. You're not feeling well. Besides, it's chilly outside. Go to the gym tomorrow." Fat Boy is the guy inside me that would rather eat than exercise.

My resistance comes disguised in many different characters. I have lots of them. In addition to Fat Boy, another character is Lazy Husband. This character often says things such as, "Why didn't Kim do this or do that?" Another resistance character that runs my life is Financial Slob, who is always saying, "Why check the numbers?" After Financial Slob has his say, then Lazy Husband says, "Kim, will you check these numbers?" As you can tell, Fat Boy, Financial Slob, and Lazy Husband are close friends of mine. We are together every day. Pressfield calls it resistance. I call them my buddies.

Steven Pressfield's book is about overcoming your resistance by tapping into your creative power, your spiritual allies, your angels or muses. I would say this book is essential for entrepreneurs. It is not a book for people who simply want to get rich quick. Like *Good to Great*, *The War of Art* contains many priceless lessons, yet there is one lesson that pertains directly to this subject on giving one's gift. It comes from a chapter entitled "Professionals and Amateurs" and says:

> *Aspiring artists defeated by Resistance share one trait. They all act like amateurs. They have not yet turned pro.*
>
> *To be clear: When I say professional, I don't mean doctors and lawyers, those of "the professions." I mean the professional as an ideal. The professional in contrast to the amateur. Consider the differences.*
>
> *The amateur plays for fun. The professional plays for keeps.*
>
> *To the amateur, the game is his avocation. To the pro, it's his vocation.*
>
> *The amateur plays part-time, the professional full-time.*
>
> *The amateur is a weekend warrior. The professional is there seven days a week.*
>
> *The word* amateur *comes from the Latin root meaning "to love." The conventional interpretation is that the amateur pursues his calling out of love, while the pro does it for money. Not the way I see it. In my view, the amateur does not love the game enough. If he did, he would not pursue it as a sideline, distinct from his "real" vocation.*
>
> *The professional loves it so much he dedicates his life to it. He commits full time.*
>
> *That's what I mean when I say turning pro.*
>
> *Resistance hates it when we turn pro.*

An Overnight Success

Writing about the success of the Rich Dad series of books, a news journalist said, "This author is an overnight success. Only three other books in the history of the *New York Times* bestseller list have been on the list longer than Kiyosaki's *Rich Dad Poor Dad*. Most authors write for years and write many books and never make the *New York Times* list."

The words *overnight success* and *author* always cause me to chuckle. I do not consider myself an author and I am certainly not an overnight success. I am simply someone who found my mission. I have been working on this mission for years and have partners who share that mission. Being an author is just one of the jobs I perform in order to fulfill that mission. I really wish I did not have to write. Ever since failing English in high school at the age of 15 because I could not write, I have had a deep aversion to writing. For years I hated writing. It was the hardest thing I had to do. There are many other ways to communicate that are easier for me and I would rather do, like audio or video recordings or live appearances. In spite of this, *Rich Dad Poor Dad* has been a best-selling business book in America for many years.

Lance Armstrong has won many Tour De France races, but his biggest battle was conquering cancer at the peak of his career. In comparison, if it's cold outside, I won't go to the gym. Armstrong's level of professionalism and love of his sport are an inspiration to us all, regardless of what our game is. As he said in his book, *It's Not About the Bike,*

> I was beginning to see cancer as something that I was given for the good of others.

> All I knew was that I felt I had a mission to serve others that I'd never had before, and I took it more seriously than anything in the world.

It's Not About the Money

Another question I am asked by journalists is: "Why do you keep working? If you have all this money, why don't you just go on a permanent vacation?" Just as Lance Armstrong states, "It's not about the bike." For me, "It's not about the money." It's about the mission.

In 1974, seeing my poor dad sitting at home watching TV, a broken and broke man, I found my mission. Watching my dad sitting there, I could see the future. Not just for him, but for millions, maybe billions of people worldwide.

In the next few years, by 2015, it will become more apparent that, throughout the world, there are millions, maybe billions, of people just like my dad. These are smart, educated, hard-working people who will need government support for food, shelter, and medicine. This is a worldwide phenomenon, affecting every country in the world, even the richest of countries such as the United States, England, Japan, Germany, France, and Italy.

In 1974, I realized the problem was that too many people, like my dad, were depending upon the government for life support. My rich dad had seen the problem growing and that Social Security and Medicare were going to be massive financial problems for the United States and the world. I could see that the richest country in the world could become a country filled with poor people expecting the government to take care of them.

In 1974, when my poor dad recommended, "Go back to school and get your PhD so you can find a job with good benefits," I found my mission. At the time, I did not know that I had found my mission. All I knew was that my dad's advice—advice I used to listen to—now deeply disturbed me. Seeing my dad sitting on the couch watching TV, unemployed, smoking, and collecting his government benefits, I knew there was something terribly flawed in his advice. Times had changed, but his advice had not. I believe seeing my father in 1974 was seeing the future.

Why Doing What You Love Is Not Enough

Very often I hear people say, "I'm doing what I love." Also I hear people say, "Do what you love, and the money will follow." While this is good advice, there are also some flaws in the advice. The most obvious flaw is the use of the word "I." One's true mission is about whom you love. It is not about you. A mission is about whom you do your work for. It's not about working for yourself.

In his book, Lance Armstrong goes on to say,

I had a new sense of purpose, and it had nothing to do with my recognition and exploits on a bike. Some people won't understand this, but I no longer felt that it was my role in life to be a cyclist. Maybe my role was to be a cancer survivor. My strongest connections and feelings were with people who were fighting cancer and asking the same question I was: "Am I going to die?"

It's Not about You

Recently, a friend asked me to talk to his sister, an office manager who had just joined a network-marketing company. He said, "She read your books and has decided to take a leap into starting her own business with a network-marketing company."

"That's good," I said.

"Would you mind talking to her?" What could I say? He was a friend, so I agreed.

During her lunch break, she came by to meet with me. "So why did you join this company and decide to build your own business?" I asked.

"Oh, I'm tired of the Rat Race. I'm not getting ahead at my job. So after reading your book on the advantages of starting a network-marketing business, *The Business School for People Who Like Helping People*, I decided to take the plunge. So I gave notice at work and will be out on my own in a month."

"That's courageous," I said, acknowledging her. "Tell me how you came to choose the network-marketing company you're going to build your business with?"

"Oh, I really like their products. Their training seems good. But I really liked their compensation plan. I can make a lot of money quickly."

"Okay," I said, reserving my comments about doing it primarily for the money. "What are your plans?"

The conversation went on for about another half hour. There was not much to discuss since she had not yet started. To be fair to my friend, I suggested she call me in six months and let me know how she was doing. At that point, I thought she would have more real-world questions to ask.

Six Months of Failing

During the sixth month, she called and wanted to continue our meeting. This next meeting was not as pleasant.

"I'm not doing very well," she started. "Nobody wants to listen to me. Nobody gets it. They just close their minds the moment I mention network marketing. How can I make any money if they don't listen?"

"Have you attended the training sessions the company offers?" I asked.

"No, I don't want to," she said angrily. "All they do is pressure me to practice selling. I don't want to be pressured. They want me to bring my friends to meetings, and my friends won't come."

"Okay," I said quietly. "Have you read any books on selling or how to influence people?"

"No. I don't like to read."

"Okay, if you don't like to read, have you looked into a sales-training course?"

"No. All those guys want is my money so I refuse to give them any."

"Okay," I said. "So what do you want?"

"All I want is to work a few hours a week, make a lot of money without hassles, and have the time and money to enjoy life."

"All right," I said, now beginning to chuckle to myself.

"So tell me what I should do," she said, flashing her frustration at me.

"Go see if you can get your job back," I suggested.

"Are you saying I can't build a business?" she demanded.

"No, I am not saying that."

"So what are you saying?" she demanded. "You're supposed to be the smart guy, the guy who writes all these best-selling books. Tell me what you see in me. I'm strong. I can take it."

"Okay," I said in a more serious tone. "Have you noticed how many times you have used the word 'I'?"

"No," she replied. "Tell me how many times I have used the word 'I' and what the use of it means to you."

"Well, I heard you say,

- 'I'm not doing well.'

- 'I don't want to attend training classes.'

- 'I don't want to read.'

- 'I refuse to give any money.'"

"So I say 'I' a lot. So what?" As gently as I could, I said, "Because building a business is not about you. It's about other people. It's about your team, your customers, your teachers, and how well you can serve them. You sound very self-centered, very me-, myself-, and 'I'-oriented."

Obviously, she did not like what I had to say, yet she sat back, kept quiet, and listened. I could tell she had heard what I had said and was processing it. Composing herself, she replied, "But I really do not like to read. I really do not like going to training classes. I really hate rejection. I hate closed-minded people who do not get what I am offering them. I hate this emotional pain I am going through. I hate not having a paycheck."

Nodding slowly, I softly said, "I understand. I have had to go through similar feelings. I too hate to read, hate to study, hate to train, hate to pay for advice, hate the long hours without pay. But I do it."

"Why?" she asked.

"Because I don't do it for me. My work is not about me. It's about them."

"So you study because you want to do better for them, your customers?"

"Yes," I replied. "Not just my customers. I study, train, and practice hard for their families, for their community, and for a better world. It's not about me or about the money. It's about being of service."

"Well, I want to be of service, too," she blurted out. "I'm trying to help people."

"Yes, I can tell you are. You have a good heart. The problem is, you must first qualify to serve."

"Qualify? What do you mean by qualify?"

"Well, medical doctors spend years in medical school qualifying to serve their patients. I do not know of anyone who has quit a job as an office manager and the next day is in the operating room performing eye surgery. Do you?"

"No," she said, shaking her head. "So that is why I need to read, train, and practice. It's not about me. It's about being better able to serve other people."

Our discussion went on for about an hour more. She did have a very good heart and sincerely did want to serve people. She simply needed to take time to gain the skills required to be better at serving people. Explaining to her the differences between P-Thinking, A-Thinking, T-Thinking, and C-Thinking people, I told her I thought she was gaining invaluable P-Thinking people skills from her network-marketing company. As she left, I said to her, "Dealing with people is the hardest part of any business."

The conversation went to the book *Good to Great*, and we discussed how greatness was a choice, not luck or chance. To encourage her to continue, I said, "Your company is not training you to be good, but to be great at dealing with people. That is a priceless skill and a skill essential to be of service to your fellow human beings. But you and only you can make that choice to be great. Most people are happy just to be good, because being good is all they need to serve themselves."

As she left, she asked, "So not all people are in business to serve other people?"

"That is my experience. Too many people go to work simply to make money. A few people go to work to be of service. Different people, different missions."

In the next chapter we will go into how to build a team and how to deal with different people with different missions. It is a very important chapter because people come to work for different reasons. If their reasons are not aligned to the mission of the business, the results are often chaos and losses of time and money. Many businesses fail simply because in business there are different people with different missions.

The Power of a Mission

In Vietnam, I witnessed firsthand a third-world nation beat the most powerful nation in the world, simply because its fighting forces had a stronger sense of mission. I see the same thing in business today. We have all seen smaller entrepreneurial companies such as Microsoft, Apple, Google, and Amazon blast past big stodgy blue-chip companies, making the young entrepreneurs far richer than older corporate executives climbing the corporate ladders. Today, while blue-chip corporate executives are becoming millionaires, youthful entrepreneurs are becoming billionaires. As in Vietnam, it's not a matter of the size of the business. It's a matter of the size of the mission. That is why I have dedicated so much time to this subject.

Earlier in this book, I wrote about the three ten-year phases of my development. Once again, they are:

1. 1974 to 1984: Learning years

2. 1984 to 1994: Earning years

3. 1994 to 2004: Giving-back years

In 1974, my mission was simply to master the B-I Triangle™. My mission was to learn. It was a dark period of life. I was often broke and depressed. It was the mission that kept me going. There were months on end that nothing seemed to work. Yet the memory of my dad sitting on his couch watching TV kept me going. I was not learning for me. I was learning for my dad and people like my dad throughout the world.

Around 1980, my world became brighter. Money was once again rolling in. I had learned many lessons about the B-I Triangle™, especially the five levels from cash flow to product. In 1980, we shipped our factories offshore because it was cheaper to manufacture in Korea and Taiwan. On one of our trips, I saw firsthand what a real-world sweatshop was. I saw kids stacked above kids on mezzanines, manufacturing my products that were making me rich.

At the time, I was manufacturing nylon wallets, bags, and hats for rock bands. We were selling our legally licensed products at rock concerts and record stores throughout the world. I was back on top again, but the sight of those kids in sweatshops haunted me.

I knew my days as a manufacturing entrepreneur were over. Besides, I realized my mission to learn was changing. I knew it was time to move on.

In December 1984, Kim and I moved to California. That began the worst year of our life. I wrote about this period of time in the book, *Rich Dad's CASHFLOW Quadrant*. My mission was similar, but it had evolved. Now my mission was to find my gift and develop it. It was also to earn money and create wealth from my gift.

Passion is different from love. Passion is a combination of love and anger. At that time, I was in love with learning and still angry at the school system. Taking my passion, Kim and I became students of education and how people learned. We spent 1985 traveling with different great teachers, such as Tony Robbins, and studying the way they taught. Once a week, we were helping Tony teach people to walk across 2,000-degree hot coals. It was a great education to help people go beyond their fears and their limiting thoughts.

After a year with Tony and other teachers, Kim and I began to teach entrepreneurial skills along with Blair Singer, author of the Rich Dad Advisor books, *Sales Dogs* and *The ABCs of Building a Business Team That Wins* (re-released as *Team Code of Honor* in 2012).

Blair and I still laugh to this day about our first workshop. He and I flew to the island of Maui to do the workshop, and only two people showed up. Even though it was a dismal start for our new business, we went on to form the Business School for Entrepreneurs and Business School for Investors. Five years later in 1990, we were filling rooms with hundreds of people, teaching the business and investing principles of my rich dad. By 1994, Kim and I were financially free. Blair went on to form his own corporate training business. Most important, I had found my gift, which is teaching, but not the same kind of teaching that my poor dad was trained to teach.

In 1994, I retired and began to work on developing the *CASHFLOW*® game and writing *Rich Dad Poor Dad*. Our third mission had begun to give back what we had been given in the form of financial and business education. Our mission was to serve more people, and once we did that, the money poured in like magic, almost from day one.

Kim and I still chuckle about the credit-card company that called us because we had too much business. After doing one talk over a weekend, orders started pouring in. The credit-card company tried to shut us down because they were certain we were selling drugs or weapons because we had processed so much business after one event. The president of the bank told us, "I cannot believe a new business can generate so much cash so quickly." Little did he know that it was the power of the mission and the three types of money—competitive, cooperative, and spiritual money—that were causing the phone to ring.

I sincerely believe the worldwide success of The Rich Dad Company is not due to Kim and me as individuals, but as people dedicated to our missions in life. When we founded The Rich Dad Company, we did not need to work. It was not about needing a job. It was not about needing money. It was about answering a higher calling. It was about doing a job that needed to be done. If it had been just about the money, there are easier things Kim and I could have done.

If our success was luck, then it was spiritual luck. There is no other way to explain it. There simply has been too much magic and too much good fortune to be attributed to merely the combined business skills of the two of us. Steven Pressfield, in his book, *The War of Art*, says, "A process is set in motion by which inevitably and infallibly, heaven comes to our aid. Unseen forces enlist in our cause; serendipity reinforces our purpose." Lance Armstrong says, "It's not about the bike."

Your Mission Starts at Your Core

Before you quit your job, remember the three kinds of money and that one type of money is not better than the other. For example, competitive money is not better or worse than cooperative or spiritual money.

Competition has its place in business. Competition keeps prices down and quality up. It keeps business people sharp and keeps us on our toes. Without competition, there would be fewer new products or life-changing innovations. Without competition, we would be approaching a socialist, centrally controlled type of economy. Without competition, there would be less need or incentive for entrepreneurs.

If you are about to become an entrepreneur, your first mission is to master the B-I Triangle™, especially the levels from cash flow up through product. If you do not learn the B-I Triangle and continually work on mastering the levels and if you are not competitive, you might not survive.

If you are not competitive, you will find it difficult to be cooperative and to work for cooperative money. In the game of business, it is tough being cooperative with poor people or poor companies. It's like playing football with a teammate who has a broken leg.

As stated in an earlier chapter, the B-I Triangle actually applies to all four quadrants of the CASHFLOW Quadrant®. For example, people in the E quadrant also have a B-I Triangle. If they are having financial challenges, it makes it easier to diagnose their financial challenge by simply looking at their private lives through the B-I Triangle. For example, many employees struggle financially simply because they are weak at the cash-flow level. Even if you give them a raise, their weakness at that level will keep them financially poor.

The Marine Corps did teach me that the mission of the organization starts at the core, in the soul of the organization. Without integrity to a mission, an organization does not have a soul. The Rich Dad Company team practices what we preach and lives our company mission. All employees are encouraged to start their own business or investment portfolios so that one day they can leave the company for good. We do not just want loyal employees. We want loyal employees who have a plan to become financially free and leave the company. We do not want our good workers to leave, but we celebrate their becoming financially free, because that is the mission of The Rich Dad Company.

So before you quit your job, remember that your mission starts at your core, in your soul, felt in your heart, and spoken through your actions—not just your words.

RICH DAD'S
ENTREPRENEURIAL LESSON #7

The Scope of the Mission Determines the Product

Chapter Seven

HOW TO GO FROM SMALL BUSINESS TO BIG BUSINESS

"Why do most small businesses remain small?" I asked.

"Good question. They remain small because there are weaknesses in their B-I Triangle™," answered rich dad. "It's tough going from the S quadrant to the B quadrant if the B-I Triangle is not strong."

After the Wreckage

There is a saying that goes, "Hindsight is 20/20." While that is true, there is some hindsight that is clearer than others. Visual aids such as the B-I Triangle and the CASHFLOW Quadrant® not only helped me see forward when designing a business, but also assisted me in seeing backward. After the crash of my nylon surfer-wallet business, having the CASHFLOW Quadrant and the B-I Triangle as visual aids was like having eyeglasses or a magnifying glass when combing through the wreckage of the business.

It was obvious that success and incompetence wiped us out. Yet, there were deeper, darker factors that caused us to crash. Being honest with myself and looking at the CASHFLOW Quadrant, it became crystal clear why we crashed. The real cause was youthful arrogance. Having a successful business early in life was like giving a kid a Corvette and a six-pack of beer and then saying, "Drive safely."

In 1976, my best friend, Larry, and I were in the E quadrant, working for Xerox as salespeople. Because we were tops in sales, we thought we knew all the answers. In our business plan, we thought we could pull an Evel Knievel and jump the Grand Canyon on a motorcycle. That means we thought we would take a shortcut to the B quadrant. Instead of going from E to S, our plan was to rev up our motorcycles and jump from E to B. Instead of climbing down the canyon from E to S, and then climbing up the other side from S to B, we decided to leap the canyon. Even Evel Knievel was smart enough to make the leap with a parachute attached to his motorcycle. We didn't.

Instead of being Evel Knievel, we looked like Wile E. Coyote chasing the Road Runner over the edge of a cliff and out into space before realizing there is nothing but air below his feet. Somewhere between 1978 and 1979, we realized we had nothing but air below us. We almost made it to the B quadrant. In fact, we touched the edge of it, but it was the weakness of our B-I Triangle™ that sent us crashing into the valley. It was not pretty and it was painful. Today, every time I see a Road Runner and Wile E. Coyote cartoon, I know how the coyote feels. Beep! Beep!

Crashes Are Good if You Survive

Between 1979 and 1981, I felt like I was the NTSB, the National Transportation Safety Board, inspecting the wreckage of an airplane. My partners had moved on to other businesses and two new partners took their place. One of them, my brother Jon, was a strong business partner as well as a tremendous moral support. Together, we went through the wreckage and rebuilt a new but smaller business. We went from B back to S.

In 1981, our downsized company entered a joint venture with a local radio station. Together with the radio station, we created a merchandising brand named "98 Rock." The star product was a black T-shirt with a splashed paint logo of red and white, screaming "98 Rock FM Honolulu." In Honolulu, our 98 Rock shops had thousands of kids lining up to buy tens of thousands of T-shirts and other accessories.

The product line soon went worldwide, doing especially well in Japan. Seeing a little 98 Rock shop in Tokyo with thousands of

Japanese kids in line to buy the products brought smiles back to our faces, smiles that had not been there for a number of years. When I told rich dad about our worldwide success, he reminded me, "The process will give a glimpse of your future, but you must be faithful to the process." Although I was not out of the woods, I knew I was getting closer to my goal. The process, although tough, was working.

The "98 Rock" craze lasted about 18 months. It made a lot of money. It was through this one marketing campaign that I was able to pay back over $700,000 to my creditors and pay off my back taxes. At the end of the fad, I was financially back to zero. Although still without money, my B-I Triangle™ skills were stronger, my confidence was back, I had turned bad luck into good luck, I did not have to declare bankruptcy, and I had caught a glimpse of the good life—my future at the end of the process.

In 1981, an agent for the rock band, Pink Floyd, called. He had heard of our success with 98 Rock merchandise and wanted us to work with them on the rerelease of their album, *The Wall*. Obviously, we jumped at the opportunity. Once again, our small company was growing into a big company. With this growth, the strength of our company's B-I Triangle was being tested again.

Our joint venture with Pink Floyd's merchandise was successful. Soon other bands came to us and, without really planning it, our little company in Honolulu was solidly in rock-and-roll merchandising. When Duran Duran and Van Halen joined our list of rock bands, the business exploded.

Simultaneously, around 1982, MTV was launched. That meant rock and roll was back, disco was dead, and once again our systems were overstressed. We were in the right place at the right time in the right business. The problem was, we could no longer keep up with demand. We also knew we could no longer produce products in America. The costs of government regulations, labor, labor laws, and factory space were too much for a little company. In order to expand, it was much more economical to move our manufacturing to Asia.

The three partners worked day and night expanding into Asia. It was about six months of hard work—not 24/7 but at least 20/7. I was virtually living in New York or San Francisco. Dave, our other partner, was in Taiwan and Korea, and my brother kept the Honolulu operations going. Operating in time zones that spanned half the globe, we were constantly on the phone (before cell phones and email) staying in touch and building a bigger B-I Triangle™. With an expanded B-I Triangle, the money once again poured in.

Occasionally I would stop in and see rich dad. During this period of time, we were not on the best of terms. He was still angry because he thought I had not listened to his advice just before the crash of the original wallet business. Although not happy with me, he was still very giving with his time and advice. Even when I reported that our new wallet business had been rebuilt and I had learned a lot from the process, he remained a little grumpy.

In hindsight, rebuilding the business was a priceless experience. My two new partners and I had all learned a lot and had grown up a lot. We were less flaky. We were smarter business people and our cash flow was the proof. Our new B-I Triangle was not leaking or collapsing. It was holding its own.

One day, my partner Dave suggested I go with him to Korea and Taiwan to see our operations. Since I had only been in San Francisco and New York during the expansion period, I had not gone to Asia to see our factories. As stated in an earlier chapter, it was on this trip to Asia that I saw the kids in sweatshops, and my career as a manufacturer ended.

Mission Accomplished

On the plane ride back from Asia to Hawaii, I realized that my mission was accomplished. Sitting in my seat, I began looking back at the process. As if it were only yesterday, I remember deciding to join the Xerox Corporation to learn how to sell in 1974. My mind also brought back memories of the day in 1976 when my friend Larry and I decided to start the nylon surfer-wallet business part-time. In 1978, I was number one in sales at Xerox and our surfer-wallet business was being written up in *GQ*, *Runner's World*, and *Playboy*.

Larry and I left Xerox to run our tiny business full-time. I recalled all the high times and then the crash. My emotions sank as I remembered how badly I felt when I told my family, my creditors, and the tax department that we were shutting the business down. I remembered the lessons from rich dad during this period. A smile crossed my face when I thought of Dave, my brother Jon, and I agreeing to rebuild the business and our success with 98 Rock, and then with MTV and rock and roll. Now the business was strong and it was time to move on. My mind kept saying, "Stay. It's now time to make a lot of money. You're back on top again. Why leave now? You're just about to get rich. The hard work is done. Your dreams will come true." Yet in my heart, I knew it was time to move on.

Deciding to move on was tough, especially with the money beginning to pour in. I struggled for months with the conflict between my head and my heart. Many times when I received my paycheck and bonus check, I definitely wanted to stay. Yet, I knew my mission to learn the fundamentals of the B-I Triangle™ had been accomplished. I could now be competitive in the business world. The problem was I did not like what I had to do to stay competitive. I did not want to employ kids in horrible conditions that would probably scar many of them for life. In late 1983, I let Dave and my brother, Jon, know that I was leaving the business. I asked for no financial compensation. I had received more than I wanted.

Meeting Kim

Just as I was preparing to make these changes in my life, I met Kim. Still the disco duck of Waikiki, I had met her months earlier, but she would not have anything to do with me. It must have been the long-collared shirts and disco boots. It did not bother me, since Waikiki was full of beautiful young women.

For some reason, after I returned from Asia, Kim came back into my thoughts. I asked her out again, and she turned me down again. This went on for six months. I would run into her, talk to her, ask her out, and she would turn me down. I would call her, and she would turn me down. I sent flowers, and she turned me down. Again and again, she turned me down. I tried every sales tactic I learned in sales training on her. I tried the puppy-dog close, the Colombo close, the "assume the sale and close" close, but none of them worked.

Finally, out of tricks from my sales bag, I stopped being a disco-duck salesperson and applied what I had learned from the marketing classes I had been taking at night. In marketing, a rule of thumb is to do your market research first. With my marketing cap on instead of my sales cap, I began asking around to find out who this woman named Kim really was. In marketing, it is called "knowing your customer."

The first person I asked was a guy who knew her from work. When I began asking questions, all he did was laugh. "You don't have a prayer," he said. "Do you know how many guys are after her? She has cards, flowers, and phone calls from guys like you all day. She probably does not know who you are." He was not helpful so I kept digging.

Finally, I was having lunch with a female friend of mine and I mentioned I was not getting far on my market-research project, code name "Kim." Phyllis cracked up after she heard my story. "Don't you know who her best girlfriend is?"

"No. I don't."

Laughing hysterically, Phyllis said, "Her best friend is Karen, your old girlfriend."

"What?" I said. "You're kidding me."

"No, I am not," laughed Phyllis.

Giving Phyllis a big hug and kiss, I ran out the door and back to the office. I had a phone call to make—to Karen.

The split between Karen and me had not been the most pleasant, so I had some patching up to do. After I had made a few belated apologies, Karen listened to the story of my six-month pursuit of Kim. She, too, laughed her head off.

Finally composing herself, she asked, "So what do you want me to do?"

Taking off my marketing cap and putting on my salesperson's cap, I asked for what every salesperson is trained to ask for from a satisfied customer. I asked for a referral.

"You want what?" screamed Karen. "You want a referral from me? You want me to recommend to her that she go out with you? You've got your nerve."

"Well, that is why I was number one in sales," I said as a joke.

Karen did not laugh. "Okay," she said, "I'll talk to her. But I warn you, that is all I am going to do. No more favors."

Karen did talk to Kim and gave me an excellent referral. About six weeks later, our calendars finally cleared and we finally had our first date on February 19, 1984.

A New Process Begins

Our date was a table overlooking the beach and a simple walk along a white sand beach with a bottle of champagne. I did not have much money, so that was about as romantic a date as I could think of for a good price. Sitting on the beach at the foot of Diamond Head, Kim and I talked until the sun came up. We had a lot of catching up to do.

That night she told me about her life, and I talked about mine. When the subject of work came up, I told her about rich dad and his lessons. She had been a business major in college and was very interested in rich dad's B-I Triangle™ and the process of becoming an entrepreneur. Sitting on the sand at the water's edge in the moonlight, talking to the most beautiful woman I had ever known about business, was like being in heaven. Most of the women the disco duck had dated up to this point were not into business. Kim was. She was very interested.

She shook her head when I told her the story of the nylon wallet business. I told her about flying high, and then the crash that followed. I told her about the kids in Asia, one stacked on top of another, four tiers of workers where there should only be one tier, inhaling toxic fumes from the paints we used. She nearly cried. Then I told her about resigning from my company because the mission was over.

With that, she took over the conversation, saying, "I'm glad you're moving on. But what are you going to do?"

Shaking my head, I replied, "I don't know. All I know is that sometimes you have to stop before you can begin again. So right now, all I am doing is stopping."

At that point, I told her about my dad who was still unemployed, taking odd jobs when he could find them. I told her about how I thought education was inadequate and not preparing kids for the real world, how schools were preparing kids to be employees not entrepreneurs, teaching kids to expect a company or the government to take care of them once their working days were over. We then discussed the future, how rich dad envisioned a coming Social Security crisis, a medical crisis, and a financial crisis in the stock market, growing bigger and bigger as the baby-boom generation aged.

"Why are you concerned?" she asked. "Why do you think the coming financial crisis is your problem?"

"I can't really say," I said. "I know that the world has a lot of problems—problems with the environment, diseases, enough food, shelter, and so on. But for me, this problem of money, poverty, and the gap between rich and poor interests me the most. I feel it in my stomach and in my heart."

The conversation shifted to Dr. Buckminster Fuller and my studies with him and how he shared the same concerns about the financial system as my rich dad. I did my best to explain to her how Dr. Fuller said the rich and powerful were playing games with money, keeping the poor and middle class constantly at the edge of financial crisis. I also told Kim about Fuller's saying that each of us had a purpose to our lives, that each of us held a vital piece of the puzzle and our job was not just to make money, but also to make this world a better place.

"It sounds like you're looking for a way to help people like your dad and people like those kids in the factory," said Kim.

I said, "That is pretty accurate. While I was in that factory, I decided it was time for me to work for the kids, instead of having the kids working for me. It is time for me to make the kids rich, rather than just myself rich."

The sun was breaking over the ocean. The young surfers were out testing the smooth glassy waves. It was time to get ready for work. We had been up all night but were full of energy. We have been together ever since.

Finding My Passion

In December 1984, Kim and I moved to California. As I have stated many times in my writings, this began the hardest period of both of our lives. The business opportunity we thought we were part of did not pan out. That left us without money, sleeping in our car for a few nights. It was a time that tested our commitment to our new business and to each other.

California was the hotbed for new models of education. Many of the hippies had grown older and were teaching seminars on some very strange and interesting subjects. The common themes were: open your mind, change your paradigms, and break through your limiting realities. Kim and I attended as many seminars as we could, gaining new ideas and observing different teaching techniques.

Earlier in this book, I wrote about attending Bob Bondurant's School of High-Performance Driving and also about working with Tony Robbins and teaching people to walk across 2,000-degree coals. As you may already know, I do not like the traditional system of education. I didn't like being taught by the fear of failing, learning to memorize all the right answers, and being afraid of making mistakes. In school, I always felt I was being programmed to do only the right things and to live in fear of living life. In school, I often felt like a butterfly caught in a spider's web, with the spider wrapping its web around and around me until I could no longer fly.

The kind of education I was looking for was an education that taught people how to break through their fears, education that would help them discover their own power within so they could walk on fire or drive a high-speed Formula-One racer. The more I studied these techniques and how we learn, how the mind works with our emotions, and how the mind affects our physical abilities, the more I wanted to learn. I became fascinated by the subject of how we as humans learn.

I discovered why I loved the Marine Corps so much. I loved Marine Corps training and flight school because it, too, was about going beyond fears and limiting thoughts. The Marine Corps was the perfect learning environment for me. The learning environment was tough and rigorous, requiring my body, mind, emotions, and soul to get through the programs.

In the Marine Corps, memorizing the right answers is not enough. Just as in the world of business, the Marine Corps is about results, not reasons. It is about actions, not words. It is a learning environment that insists that the mission be first, the team second, and the individual last. It is a learning environment that taught me to fly rather than a learning environment that clipped my wings.

Breakthrough Learning

It was dawning on me that what we were studying was what I came to call "breakthrough learning"—the type of learning that is powerful enough to cause a transformation, a paradigm shift of reality, much like how a chick must feel when it finally breaks through the shell of the egg.

During one of the learning seminars I attended, I learned about Ilya Prigogine, a person who was awarded the Nobel Prize for his research on dissipative structures. To put it into as simple an example as possible, his research proved why a child will climb on a bike, fall off, climb on, fall off, and then suddenly be able to ride. Again in the simplest of terms, under the extreme stress of falling down and getting up again and again, the stress of the process causes the child's brain to reorder. The brain goes from not knowing how to ride a bicycle to being able to ride a bicycle forever.

To me, his research verified why people who do well in school may not do well in the real world. There are many people who know what to do, but cannot do what they know. Like my dad, once they fall down, they stay down and say, "I'll never do that again." Instead of pressing on with increasing stress and frustration, they back off to reduce the stress. In many ways, it is like the chick remaining in its protective shell.

As Prigogine summarized, "Stress is the way intelligence grows." Or as rich dad would say, "Stay with the process."

How Fast Can We Learn?

Another person whose work I researched was Georgi Lozanov of Bulgaria, the pioneer of what is now called Super-Learning. Although I never took one of his classes, it is reported that he was able to teach people a complete language in one or two days. Obviously, traditional academics discredit him and his work. I began experimenting with his techniques and found out that they really do work.

One reason I disliked school so much was simply that the pace was too slow. It took too long to learn too little. Combining different teaching techniques increased the speed of learning, reduced boredom, and resulted in greater long-term retention. I began to become excited about education. What I liked most about what I was discovering was that it did not matter if you were an "A" student or an "F" student. With this method of teaching, all it took to learn was the desire to learn.

Finding My Passion

Rich dad had said to me years earlier that once you complete a process, you take the best with you and leave the rest behind. You then move on to the next process.

As Kim and I were going through this learning period, rich dad's words began to make sense. Suddenly, it dawned on me that I was beginning the best of several processes in my life. I had my experience from the process of going to school, which I really hated. Next were my experiences from the process of being a Marine pilot. Then I had my experiences from learning to be an entrepreneur with my nylon-wallet business. As tough as that nylon-wallet process was, I did have many great experiences to take with me. And now, actually becoming a student of how people learn, all my past experiences were coming together. My often-disorderly life was beginning to make sense.

Around August 1985, I found my passion. My next business was forming in my mind. From 1986 to 1994, Kim and I ran an organization that offered the Business School for Entrepreneurs and the Business School for Investors. Instead of your traditional business school, this business school had no prerequisites. We did not require scholastic records. All that was required was the will to learn and the time and money for the courses.

Employing the techniques we had learned, we were able to teach people the basics of accounting and investing—normally a six-month course—in one day. Instead of talking about business, the class actually built a business touching on all parts of the B-I Triangle™. Instead of talking about team building, each business team had to train for a triathlon. Instead of one person finishing first, it was the team that finished first that won. I do not know if you know how hard it is to get 15 people of different ages, different genders, different levels of fitness, and different mindsets to compete as a team in a contest of swimming, biking, and running. Some of the contests reminded me of scenes from Vietnam where team members were carrying other team members across the finish line. Of course, to be a real business school, we bet money. Every participant put money in the pot, and it was winner take all. A winning team of 15 could walk away with as much as $50,000 in prize money.

At our Business School for Investors, instead of talking about investing, we actually would build a stock-market trading floor. The different teams would represent different stocks and money managers. As market conditions changed, the teams had to adjust their investment strategies. Again, at the end of the school, the winning team walked away with the money.

In 1993, although the business was successful and profitable, I knew it was once again time to move on. In the summer of 1994, Kim and I sold our share of the business to our partner and retired. The passive income generated from our investments was now greater than our expenses. We were finally out of the Rat Race. We weren't rich, but we were financially free. In my book, *Rich Dad's Retire Young Retire Rich*, you will see on the back cover a picture of Kim and me sitting on horses on a hill overlooking a crystal-blue ocean. That vacation on a private island in Fiji was our reward for retiring early. Kim was thirty-seven and I was forty-seven.

Know When to Stop

In his book, *Good to Great,* Jim Collins does a whole piece on knowing when to stop. Reading his book in 2004 took me back to the times when I also stopped in 1984 and 1994. There was no clear signal, no sign from God saying, "It's time to stop." Each time, there was simply a moment when I knew the process I was in had come to an end. It was time to stop and wait for the beginning of the next process.

Many times I meet business people who want to stop, but can't stop. They cannot stop for different reasons. One common reason is that their B-I Triangle™ is weak. To cover up for the weaknesses, the owner often has to work harder or longer to make up for the weaknesses. Another reason is that the owner cannot afford to stop. Again, this is a symptom of a weakness in the B-I Triangle. Another common reason is that the owner, although successful, continues to work because he or she does not know what to do next. According to Jim Collins, a person may need to stop first, take some time off, and then look for the next thing. That is what I did. I simply stopped, let the dust settle, and waited a few years to see what would happen next.

The More People You Serve, the More Effective You Become

From 1984 to 1994, I was firmly entrenched in the S quadrant. I was not going to make any premature moves toward the B quadrant. As expected, as our success grew, so did our exhaustion. Exhaustion is what often occurs with successful people in the S quadrant. Since an S individual often does the work himself, more success means more work. An S often works for a dollar-per-hour compensation plan, and as we all know, there are only so many hours in a day.

When Kim and I stopped, it was not the hard work or long hours that caused us to stop. What was disturbing me was how few people our work was reaching. After all, only a few people actually pay money to attend seminars. And our seminars were not only expensive, but also tough like the Marine Corps. We asked people to devote ten or more days to attend one of our business schools.

Dr. Buckminster Fuller, the teacher who has had a tremendous influence on my life, often said, "The more people you serve, the more effective you become." He was not into money, but he was into being of service. Rich dad said, "One of the big differences between an S and a B is the number of customers they can handle." He also said, "If you want to be rich, simply serve more people."

By 1994, our last business school had over 350 people in the class paying $5,000 each to attend. If you do the math, the money was good. What was not good was that there were only 350 people. I knew that if I truly wanted to help those kids in Asia, I was not going to be able to do it doing things the way I was doing them. In other words, I knew it was time to stop and figure out how to go from the S quadrant to the B quadrant. Instead of trying to leap across the Grand Canyon, Kim and I were now ready to climb up the other side. It was time to go through what rich dad called "the eye of the needle."

Going through the Eye of the Needle

As most of you know, one of the problems with being self-employed in the S quadrant is the word *self.* In many cases, the self-employed person is the product, the person who is hired to do the work. When you look at the B-I Triangle™, starting from the cash-flow level on up to product, the self-employed person is in charge of everything, all the elements. In most cases, being self-employed makes it very difficult to get to the B quadrant. It can be difficult to get yourself out of the way.

Between 1984 and 1994, I was that person. I was the self in self-employed. Although I did it intentionally, the reality disturbed me. A question I often asked myself was, "How can I teach people what I have been teaching in our business schools without my personally teaching them?"

We tried training other instructors, but that process was a long, hard, tedious process. It was difficult to find people to go through the training process to become instructors. It was hard to teach other people to teach the way we taught. It's not easy to get a class of over 300 people to learn accounting and investing in one day. It was almost as tough as teaching them to walk across fire.

After selling the business in 1994, I had time to go back to my question, "How can I teach people what I have been teaching in our business schools without my teaching them?" I moved into the mountains near Bisbee, Arizona, and was secluded enough to begin working on the answer to my question. For two years I worked on the question. When I left Bisbee, I had the rough draft for *Rich Dad Poor Dad* on my Macintosh computer and a rough sketch with computations for the *CASHFLOW®* board game. I was going through the eye of the needle and moving from the S quadrant to the B quadrant.

Rich dad had learned about the eye of the needle from Sunday school. He said, "A popular Bible verse goes something like this: 'It is easier for a camel to pass through the eye of a needle than for a rich man to pass into heaven.'" Rich dad continued, modifying the verse to say, "Forget the camel. If a man can pass through the eye of a needle, he will enter a world of tremendous wealth."

Now rich dad was a very religious man and was not making fun of the verse. He was simply modifying it to create his own lesson. In business terms, what he meant was that for an entrepreneur to pass through the eye of a needle, the entrepreneur has to leave himself behind. What passes through the eye of the needle is the entrepreneur's idea, or intellectual property. Looking at the diagram below, you may better understand what rich dad meant.

There are many examples of entrepreneurs going through the eye of the needle throughout history. Here are a few:

- When Henry Ford designed his automobile to be mass-produced, he passed through the eye of the needle. Up until then, most cars were custom-ordered and hand-made.

- When Steve Jobs and his team at Apple created the iPod, the iPad, the iPhone, and iTunes, they went through the eye of the needle.

- When someone like Steven Spielberg or George Lucas creates a movie, they, too, go through the eye of the needle.

- McDonald's went through the eye of the needle by franchising their hamburger business worldwide.

- When a network marketer builds a down line of other business owners, he or she goes through the eye of the needle.

- When investors buy an asset, such as an apartment house that cash flows money into their pocket each and every month, they have gone through the eye of the needle.

- A politician who uses the media to campaign is going through the eye of the needle. A politician who goes door to door is not.

- When inventors or authors sell their invention or their book to a large company, which in return pays them royalties, they have gone through the eye of the needle.

- When I took what I had learned from rich dad and created the board game and wrote the book, I was going through the eye of the needle. I was getting myself out of the equation.

- When I created my nylon shoe-pocket wallet for runners and did not first have my idea protected by an intellectual-property attorney, I was not going through the eye of the needle. I was simply giving my idea to my competition and making them rich. They went through the eye of the needle, and I fell into the Grand Canyon. I had a great new product, but without the legal level to protect my product, the B-I Triangle™ was not complete.

The Chick Breaks through Its Shell

When I returned to Phoenix with a draft of the book and the *CASHFLOW*® board game in hand, I knew I was making my move to the B quadrant. Kim and I began to design and build a company according to the B-I Triangle. The moment we put our products in the marketplace, the heavens of abundance opened up.

The product line was officially unveiled on my fiftieth birthday, April 8, 1997. From the start of The Rich Dad Company, we had a few struggles to breathe life into the business. The main struggles we had were keeping up with demand, traveling the world to open new markets, and counting the money. In June 2000, the call from *The Oprah Winfrey Show* came, and the heavens really opened. Kim and I were leaping from S to B.

At this point, I began to better understand what rich dad meant by:

- Being true to the process

- The process will give you glimpses of a better future, just to keep you going

- The power of mastering the B-I Triangle

- Harnessing the power of the three types of money: competitive, cooperative, and spiritual money

- Going through the eye of the needle

After being on Oprah's show, I truly felt like the chick that had finally cracked through its shell. Before Oprah, no one knew me. After Oprah, regardless of where I go in the world, people stop me on the street to let me know they have read *Rich Dad Poor Dad* or played the *CASHFLOW*® games.

In 2002, I was in an antique store in Stockholm, Sweden. The owner, a very blonde Swede, was an expert in Chinese antiques. Recognizing me, he said, "I was on a buying trip to China a few months ago. While floating down the Yangtze River, I glanced into a houseboat and saw a Chinese family playing the Chinese version of your *CASHFLOW*® board game."

At that moment, I realized that I had kept my promise to those kids in the sweatshop, kids who were working to make me rich. Now my products were working for kids just like them, teaching families, people young and old, how to have money work for them, rather than working all their lives for money, and then hoping to have the government take care of them.

In February 2004, the *New York Times* did a full-page feature story about the *CASHFLOW*® game and about the hundreds of clubs forming throughout the world. Clubs were forming just to play the game and to learn what my rich dad had taught me. When I saw that article, I could not believe my eyes. I could not believe the magic. To me, having the *New York Times* writing this article was as big as being on Oprah's show.

When I saw the article, I knew that what I had learned from teaching my Business School for Entrepreneurs and Business School for Investors had been successfully transformed into a product, the *CASHFLOW*® games, that could teach what I used to teach. People were now learning the fundamentals of accounting and investing in less than a day. On top of that, many of the players have had significant breakthroughs in how they see the world. For them, the game delivered the paradigm shift, the shift from seeing the world of money as a frightening place to seeing it as an exciting place. Instead of looking for experts and blindly turning their money over to these so-called experts, through the game many people realized that they could become their own financial experts. They could take control of their own financial future. And many of them have.

Best of all, instead of personally teaching only 350 people at a time and charging them thousands of dollars, the *CASHFLOW* game was now going to them and teaching hundreds of thousands of people, many of them for free. Instead of my teaching them, they were teaching themselves, and then teaching and sharing with others.

When I saw the *New York Times* article, I knew the ten-year period from 1994 to 2004 was coming to an end. However, even though that ten-year process is complete, we know the mission continues.

Get Yourself Out of the Way

Before you quit your job, you may want to remember the lesson of this chapter. The lesson is that the scope of the mission determines the product. It is very tough making a lot of money or serving a lot of people simply by working harder physically. If you want to serve a lot of people and/or make a lot of money, you may need to get yourself out of the way and pass through the eye of the needle.

Before you quit your job, you may also want to determine if you would be happiest in the S quadrant or the B quadrant. If you want to grow into the B quadrant, remember that it takes much stronger fundamentals in the B-I Triangle™ and an even stronger team to allow you to go through the eye of the needle.

And before you quit your job, you may want to have a moment of silence in memory of the dotcom companies that failed. I believe the reason so many failed was that many of the entrepreneurs were attempting to leap from the E quadrant to the B quadrant. When the bust came, they, too, looked like Wile E. Coyote with only air beneath their feet. They did not make it through the eye of the needle.

A Winning Team

Success or failure in business has to do with work ethic, determination, and desire. Most people who make that jump have tons of all three. Yet the biggest determining factor has even more to do with learning three critical skills that will turn any business into a success.

First, in order to build a business, you have to be able to sell because Sales = Income. When income is lacking, it's usually because the owner doesn't like to, doesn't know how to, or is simply reluctant to sell. Without sales, however, you have no income. There is a myth that you have to be an attack dog to sell. Not true.

Second, in order to build a real business or network and move out of the S quadrant, you have to be able to attract, build, and motivate a great team. In the world of small business, everyone on that team has to be willing to sell, regardless of their position in the company.

In order to make that happen, the third element becomes critical. That is your ability to teach others in the business how to sell, how to be great team players, and how to succeed. It is this skill that ensures growth, profit, and longevity.

The sad fact is that most business owners are never taught how to do any of those things. As a matter of fact, most of us are conditioned to believe that sales is a nasty task, that if you want things done right you have to do them yourself and that teaching is what you experienced in school.

When we work in business, the very first thing we do to increase income is to help people establish what we call the Code of Honor. The Code is a simple set of rules that turns even ordinary people into a championship team—a team that not only sells, but is hungry to learn and enforces an incredible level of accountability for personal conduct, performance, and numbers. It articulates the behaviors that are critical for success, and it demands the agreement of all team members to play that way.

Most people would like to be the best that they can be. As a business owner, you have to create the environment or context that will make that happen. It's not only something that you can learn, but it's something that will make you successful. Many times in business, it's not what you deliver but how you deliver it that makes the biggest difference. It's the strength and commitment of your team and their passion to promote and serve others that determine your reputation, your success, and your cash flow.

Blair Singer
Rich Dad Advisor and author of
Sales Dogs and
Team Code of Honor

Choosing the Right Entity

Few people appreciate it, but choosing the right entity structure for your business is just as important as choosing the right partner for your business.

If you go into business with the wrong person, your efforts may be doomed from the start. The wrong person may too freely spend your money, may obligate the company to contracts it cannot fulfill, and may alienate coworkers before the first product or service is ever delivered. The wrong partner can leave you unprotected and waste all of your efforts and energy.

Likewise, choosing the wrong legal structure can also lead directly to failure. Starting out, you want to have as much asset and legal protection as possible. But by choosing a sole proprietorship or a general partnership, bad entities that offer no protection whatsoever, you stand to lose everything you build into your business, along with all of your personal assets. Plaintiffs and their attorneys love to see businesses operated as sole proprietorships and general partnerships because they can reach both business and personal assets when they bring a claim. They have free rein to reach all of your assets.

Instead, use a good entity such as a C-Corporation, S-Corporation, limited liability company, or limited partnership. These entities protect your personal assets from attack against the business. And like the right partner, the right entity will help you advance your protection and future prospects.

Garrett Sutton, Esq.
Rich Dad Advisor, author of
Buying and Selling a Business
Start Your Own Corporation
Writing Winning Business Plans, and
The ABCs of Getting Out of Debt

RICH DAD'S
ENTREPRENEURIAL LESSON #8

Design a Business
That Can Do Something
That No Other Business
Can Do

Chapter Eight
WHAT IS THE JOB OF A BUSINESS LEADER?

The Business Leader

"What is the business leader's most important job?" I asked rich dad.

"Well, there are many jobs that are very important. It would be hard to say if any one job is more important than the other. Instead of just one job, I can tell you what I think my eight most important jobs are."

The following is rich dad's list:

1. Clearly define the mission, goals, and vision of the company.

2. Find the best people and forge them into a team.

3. Strengthen the company on the inside.

4. Expand the company on the outside.

5. Improve the bottom line.

6. Invest in research and development.

7. Invest in tangible assets.

8. Be a good corporate citizen.

"What happens if the leader cannot perform those jobs?" I asked.

"You need to change leaders," said rich dad. "Besides, if the leader cannot do these things, the company will probably disappear anyway. That is why most new companies are gone within ten years."

Only a Mission

Over the years, I have met many people with an extremely strong sense of mission. I have had people come up to me and say things such as:

- "I want to save the environment."

- "My invention will eliminate the need for fossil fuels."

- "I want to start a charity that provides shelter for runaway kids."

- "My technology is what the world has been waiting for."

- "I want to find a cure for that disease."

While their care and concern may be genuine, many of these good-hearted people fail to fulfill their mission simply because all they have is a mission. If you were to look at their life skills through the context of the B-I Triangle™, it would look like this.

A Lack of Business Skills

Earlier in this book, I mentioned that many people spend years in school or at work developing skills that are not relevant or important to the B-I Triangle™. I mention the example of a schoolteacher, who may have years of education and teaching experience, yet those years of education may not transfer to the B-I Triangle if that person decides to become an entrepreneur. That person simply lacks business skills.

When I left the Marine Corps in 1974, I too was in that predicament. By 1974, I had two professions. My first profession was as a licensed ship's officer, licensed to sail any ship of unlimited tonnage throughout the world. I could have made a lot of money with this profession. The problem was, I did not want to be a ship's officer anymore.

My second profession was that of a military pilot with great training and years of experience. Many of my friends went to work for the airlines or with police and fire departments as pilots. I could have done the same thing, except that I no longer wanted to fly.

In 1974 when I returned home to see my dad struggling financially, I suspected that I had found my new mission, or at least a problem worth solving. The problem was, all I had was a mission. When you look at the B-I Triangle, there are levels for people specially trained in accounting, law, design, marketing, and systems. There are not levels that say ship's officer or pilot. So, I was just like the many people I mentioned above—people with a mission, but with a lack of real business skills.

What I did have going for me was that I had years of apprenticeship to rich dad. I had worked in all aspects of the B-I Triangle through his businesses. So I did have some business experience, but only as a kid. At least I knew that a business was a system of systems, and I understood the importance of the B-I Triangle as a business structure.

Complaining to Rich Dad

One day I complained to rich dad that I had almost no marketable skills that applied to the B-I Triangle. Pointing to the Team side of the B-I Triangle, I complained that no major corporation would hire me to be on their team. I whined on about not having a formal education at any of the levels. After I was through complaining, I looked up at rich dad for what I hoped would be a sympathetic answer. All he said was, "Neither do I."

A mission is all that rich dad started with.

What a Leader Does

A leader's job is to change the company to allow it to grow and serve more people. If the leader cannot change the company, the leader keeps the company small and the company may begin to shrink.

Once again, I use the B-I Triangle™ to further clarify this point.

When I was in the S quadrant, our products were the Business School for Entrepreneurs and the Business School for Investors. The problem with the business was that I was too much a part of the product as well as the rest of the B-I Triangle. If I was going to be a leader, I needed to stop and completely redesign the business. Trying to fix a poorly designed business while the business is running is like trying to change a flat tire while the car is still moving. That is why Kim and I stopped and took two years off before we started a new business.

Building a New B-I Triangle™

In 1996 when I came out of the mountains around Bisbee, Arizona, all I had were pencil sketches of the *CASHFLOW*® game board, a rough draft of *Rich Dad Poor Dad* in my computer, and a simple two-page business plan. As the sole employee of my yet-to-be-formed company, I knew my next step was to find the right people and put a team together.

Sketching the game board was the easy part. Finding someone who could engineer the information systems required to make the game work was the first step. The game had to be engineered to literally change the way people think about money. At that time, there was only one person I knew who had such a mind. That was an old friend named Rolf Parta, fondly known as Spock. We call him Spock because he looks like Leonard Nimoy of Star Trek fame. He also happens to be as smart as the character Nimoy played.

This is where the four types of thinking are important. For this phase of the business, I brought the C-Thinking and P-Thinking to the project. I was creative enough to sketch a crude game-board design, and I understood how people learned from my ten years of teaching. Spock brought the T-Thinking and A-Thinking to the project. As a trained CPA with an MBA, and a former banker with an extremely high IQ, Spock lives in a world of his own. Very few people can carry on a conversation with him. He speaks a dialect of English I doubt anyone else understands.

Arriving at his home, I spread my crude sketches and diagrams on his dining-room table. Doing my best to communicate by words, gestures, and pointing at my sketches, Spock and I finally began to converse. It is tough being the creative and people side of the project speaking to what I hoped would be the technical and analytical side.

Finally, about an hour into the discussion, Spock's eyes lit up. He was beginning to understand the people and creative side. "Why do people need this game?" he asked. "This is common sense."

Chuckling, I replied, "To you, it's common sense. You have an MBA. You're a CPA, and a former banker. So to you, this is common sense. But to the average person, this is a foreign language. For many people, this is a radically new way of thinking."

Spock grinned. The points on his ears grew a little longer. "Give me three months, and I'll give you what you want." We agreed upon a price for his services, shook hands, and I left feeling confident that I had found the right person for the task.

Three months later and after much interaction with me, he had all the complex mathematical equations done. I had done my part and made better crude sketches. Together, Kim, Spock, and I played the game. Surprisingly, the game ran well. It was a tough game, but the numbers worked, the lessons were revealed, and we were happy.

The next person I went to see was an intellectual-property attorney to begin the process of filing for patents, trademarks, and other legal fences to protect my intellectual property.

Spock went back to work with his A-Thinking cap on, using his analytical mind this time, and began back-testing the game on a computer. He ran the game through 150,000 different simulations without a failure. When he handed me his pages of mathematical computations, he was grinning from ear to ear. The challenge of the project had made him very happy.

To this day, I have no idea what the math on those pages meant, but when I turned those same pages over to my attorney, he grinned just like Spock. I felt like I was in school again. The two "A" students were going over test papers and enjoying it, and I—the "C," "D," and occasional "F" student—wondered what they were so excited about.

As you may have already guessed, I was now building a new B-I Triangle™. As entrepreneurs, Kim and I were clear on our mission. Now, as leaders of the project and using the five levels inside the Triangle as a guide, we were now putting together a team.

After about a month, my attorney called and said, "You can now move forward and show your game to other people. We do not have a patent yet, but I have filed the application and you've staked your claim. You still need to have people sign confidentiality agreements before they see your product."

As you may recall, this is the step I left out when I created the runner's shoe-pocket wallet. Within weeks after inventing the product, I began selling the shoe pocket without protection. In less than three months, our competitors were selling my creation. It was a devastating mistake. But learning my lesson from that mistake was about to pay off in a very, very, big way.

The Big Test

For the next few weeks, Kim, Spock, and I worked to get our prototype games ready. We had played the game with a number of our friends and the game worked well. The reason the game worked well is that all of our friends are professional investors. Now we were about to beta test the game. (A beta test is a trial run to see if the game works with the average player.)

The game at that stage was just rough sketches on heavy butcher paper, and we used different-caliber bullets as game pieces. The bullets worked well because their weight helped keep the paper down.

We reserved a hotel conference room, enough for about 20 people, and then began calling people, mostly strangers, to come and play. You have no idea how hard that was. When people found out the game was an educational game about investing and accounting, most people found an excuse to not be there.

"Does it require math?" asked one person.

When I said, "Yes," he hung up.

The Game Is Played

One bright Saturday morning, in walked nine people. One who agreed to be there simply did not show up.

After a few niceties, the game was on, and it went on and on and on. There were two tables—one table with four people and one with five. After about three hours, one person raised her hand to signal she had won her game. The game had worked—for one person—and the game went on and on and on.

Finally at about 1:00 p.m., we shut the game down. Frustration was so high, I thought fights were about to break out. No one else had gotten out of the Rat Race. No one else had won the game. As people left, many politely shook my hands, but no one said much. Most just gave me a strange look and left.

Decision Time

After packing up our boxes, Kim, Spock, and I had a debriefing session. "Maybe it's too hard," I said. Kim and Spock nodded.

"But one person got out of the Rat Race. She won the game," said my perpetually optimistic wife, Kim.

"Yeah, but most people didn't win," I moaned. "They didn't get out of the Rat Race. They didn't learn anything. All they did was get frustrated."

"I did my best to make it simple," said Spock. "I don't know if I can make it any easier without losing the objectives for playing the game."

"Well, let's get the boxes into the car and go home. Kim and I leave for Hawaii tomorrow. We'll have to decide if we go forward with this project or shut it down."

For the next week, Kim and I would get up, have our coffee, and walk on the beach. One morning I would be overly enthusiastic, ready to continue with the project. The next morning, I would awake depressed, ready to shut the project down. This went on for a week. It was a horrible vacation.

The reason I spend so much time writing about this period is that it was a very tough time for me. When people say they have fears about taking risks and going forward on a project, well, so do I. Kim and I were in turmoil during this period of time. It was go or no go. It was put up or shut up. It was live our mission, or just go back to making money.

Kim and I both believed that many of the important lessons that rich dad had taught me had been transferred into our new game. We knew we had to move forward. Spock, Kim, and I decided to go through the eye of the needle. We had transferred this knowledge I had learned from rich dad and placed it in a tangible product.

This took place in the summer of 1996. Kim and I then went forward and hired a graphic artist to bring the game to life. He then shipped his work to a game-manufacturing company in Canada. In November 1996, the commercial version of the game was played at a friend's investment seminar in Las Vegas, Nevada. The game worked. Participants loved the game. The paradigm shifts we wanted were happening. Immediately, we flew to Singapore to another friend's investment workshop. Once again, the game did its magic.

Trademarks and Trade Dress

We then worked on the graphics that help identify the Rich Dad brand. You may notice that most of our products have a similar theme, look, and feel. We use are specific colors—purple, grey, black and a few secondary colors. People associate the color schemes with The Rich Dad Company. If people infringe upon our trade dress or trademarks, which people often do, our legal team begins talking to them. Our trademarks and trade dress are assets called "intellectual property" that have great value all over the world. In China, they call Rich Dad "the Purple Storm."

The Business Takes Off

Once the business was put together, the company began to take off. Orders started flying through the door. Cash flowed in. All debts were immediately paid off, and soon the company was bursting at the seams. We were forced to buy an office building to house a growing company. *Rich Dad Poor Dad* made the *Wall Street Journal* and the *New York Times* bestseller lists, one of the few books on the lists not published by the large publishing houses.

Publishing houses started calling, offering us a lot of money to sign with them. Oprah's show called and in the summer of 2000, after I was on her program, the company really exploded. Almost overnight, we became an international success.

How to Expand a Business

There are many ways a business can expand.

1. **Replicate the entire B-I Triangle™**
    Basically, once you work the bugs out of the first business, you open more of them. Many retailers and restaurants expand this way. In many cities, there are restaurants that have three or four successful stores located throughout the city. In order to grow bigger, the leader may need to change leaders. Often, the owner will sell to a bigger company and start over again.

2. **Franchise**
    McDonald's is the most famous example of expansion via franchising.

3. **Take the company public through an IPO**

   With funds from places like Wall Street, the company can tap into a virtually unlimited supply of money as long as the company keeps on expanding.

4. **License the products**

   This is the way we designed The Rich Dad Company to expand. Licensing is basically allowing another business to produce your products. As our success grew, our licensing, which is the legal level of the business, expanded to 42 different languages in over 55 countries. It costs us no money to produce or store the books. We do not need a giant warehouse, an extensive sales force, or a large inventory to ship product around the world.

The Single-Tactic, Multiple-Strategy Plan

My training as a military officer required that we know the difference between a tactic and a strategy. In very simple terms, a tactic is what you do. A strategy is the plan on how to get the tactic done.

One of my military-science instructors was adamant about the importance of using a single-tactic, multiple-strategy plan of warfare to win. He would say, "A military leader must focus on one objective or tactic. He must only want to do one thing. Everything else is a strategy on how to get that one tactic done." He would then use examples of military conflict after military conflict that was won by the leader that had the best strategies focused on a single tactic.

When I entered the business world, I carried his lessons with me. Soon I began to see that companies that used the single-tactic, multiple-strategy type of planning were companies that won in business. For example, Domino's Pizza started with a single tactic to beat its competition. To distinguish itself in the pizza wars, Domino's designed a company around a single tactic. That tactic was to promise "pizza in 30 minutes or less." An entire business was designed around that single promise, a single tactic. To make that single tactic a reality, the company then had multiple strategic plans. Once Domino's entered the marketplace, it immediately began taking market share from its competitors. Competitors such as Pizza Hut could not compete because the business was not designed to meet such a promise. To combat Domino's, Pizza Hut increased advertising—the communications level—to announce new and different types of pizza—the product level. The pizza wars were on. Pizza Hut was fighting with a better product. Domino's was fighting with a guaranteed faster delivery.

If you have read Jim Collins's book, *Good to Great*, you will notice that many of the great companies have single tactics. Jim Collins does not call it a single-tactic, multiple-strategy way of winning. Instead, he calls it "the hedgehog principle."

In his book, he uses Walmart's single tactic—the lowest price for good products—as the reason it beats its competitors who have multiple tactics and even more strategies. In other words, Walmart's competitors simply have not clearly defined their own single winning tactic. Walmart's entire business is focused on one promise, a promise customers clearly like. That means Walmart does not win in the product category. Like Domino's, it wins in the system level of the B-I Triangle™.

You may recall that Thomas Edison won the electric-light battle at the system level, not at the product level. Henry Ford also won at the system level. He simply mass-produced low-priced cars for the working family. He never promised the best-made cars. He just promised the best-priced cars, and then designed a business around his promise. McDonald's does not produce the best hamburger. Ray Kroc built a business around the idea of selling the best franchise to people who want to own a franchise.

When I was in the Arizona mountains, the very simple business plan I came up with was based upon one single tactic and three strategies. The first page of the simple two-page plan looked like this.

TACTIC: PLAY THE *CASHFLOW*® GAME

STRATEGIES: 1. WRITE A BOOK
                     2. DO AN INFOMERCIAL
                     3. TEACH INVESTMENT SEMINARS
                       USING THE GAME

On the second page, I wrote a brief plan on how I thought I could accomplish the three strategies.

The single tactic was to get as many people as possible to play the game. I knew that if I created a great game and people played it, their lives would change. They would be able to see another world of opportunity. They would be less inclined to blindly turn their money over to people they thought were experts, such as mutual-fund managers, and might be inspired to become their own financial experts.

That was it. I knew, if successful, I would make money from the strategies as well as the single tactic.

A Low-Risk Idea

The first lesson: Always have a low-risk idea or strategy to fall back on.

Rich dad taught me that whenever you start a business or invest in something, you need to have a low-risk idea. For example, when investing in real estate, if the investment paid me something each and every month, that was a low-risk investment. Even if the property did not go up in value, I was still receiving some compensation for my investment dollars.

The strategy of teaching investment seminars using the game was my low-risk idea. Since I came from the seminar business, I knew that if the other two strategies did not work and no one wanted my game, I could recoup my investment in the product development of the game simply by putting on investment seminars.

Simply put, a low-risk idea is something you know you can do.

Design A Business That Can Do Something That No Other Business Can Do

The second lesson: Design the business around a unique tactical advantage. In my plan, my tactic was to play the game so I virtually eliminated all competition. I eliminated all competition because if the legal work was strong, no one else could do what our business did. No one else has our *CASHFLOW* games. As rich dad said, "Design a business that can do something that no other business can do."

Simply put, focus all your efforts on your core strength, your unique product.

The plan worked. Once we had built the books to a certain level of success on our own, we licensed other publishers around the world to publish versions in other languages. We licensed the rights to sell certain products through infomercials. We went on the road to do investment seminars across the United States, in Australia, and in Singapore. Cash flowed in from all three strategies, as well as from the sales of the game.

When I talked about spiritual money, I really did not think we would have made as much money as we did from just our strategies. It was like magic.

More Strategies Today

Today, the tactic is the same. All of our strategies are focused on getting people to play the *CASHFLOW* games.

Today the number of strategies has increased. Today our business looks like this:

1. Books in 42 different languages

2. Games in 14 different languages

3. Network-marketing companies using our products

4. A coaching company

5. A seminar company

6. A national radio show

7. CASHFLOW clubs throughout the world

8. Digital online game initiatives

9. Curriculum initiatives including richkidsmartkid.com which offers free games and curriculum for kindergarten through 12th grade

Our company grows by adding partners who can add to our strategies. Via licensing or co-venturing, we do not have to grow the size or number of employees of The Rich Dad Company. Our company remains small, but has big partners.

Three Jobs of Leaders

At the start of this chapter, I listed a set of jobs rich dad thought were important for a leader. Once the product was developed and protected legally via patents and trademarks, Kim and I focused on the following three jobs of leaders.

1. Strengthen the company on the inside

2. Expand the company on the outside

3. Improve the bottom line

Working for Cooperative Money

Through all this very rapid growth, the company handled the expansion without a hitch. Instead of success destroying us as it did with the nylon-wallet company, The Rich Dad Company grew stronger with the growth. The company grew because we were cooperative, working for cooperative money. Every dollar that came in from our licensed strategic partners was a cooperative dollar. By cooperating instead of competing, our strategic partners get richer, and so do we. I believe our company was pretty well designed. It was designed to grow. We leveraged the talents of our team to build and protect intellectual property and then leveraged the intellectual property through licensing all over the world. We found the right team to guide us in this process.

As we grew The Rich Dad Company, we did not have the growing pains many small companies go through. We did not have cash-flow problems, space problems, or adding-employee problems. The company remained basically the same size even as we grew exponentially. What expanded was the number of strategic partners. As we grew, more and more money flowed in, and very few dollars flowed out. All my years of screwing up, correcting, and learning were paying off.

No More Glimpses

Today, instead of just a glimpse of the world I want to live in, Kim and I live in a world better than we ever dreamed of. It seems like magic, and it is magic. The money and lifestyle are great, but it is the sense of making a difference in so many lives that is the true magic. When I think back on my dad sitting unemployed in front of the TV set, the kids in the sweatshops in Asia from my wallet business, and then to the families playing *CASHFLOW*® on the Yangtze River, that is the real magic. As Dr. Buckminster Fuller would say, "It's the work of the great spirit." As Lance Armstrong says, "It's not about the bike."

The Entrepreneur's Job Is Done

Once I saw the article about the *CASHFLOW*® game in the *New York Times*, I knew my job as an entrepreneur was over. We had done our job. Kim and I had taken the business as far as we could take it. We knew it was time for a new team. In the summer of 2008, our new team took over. The team has changed, but their jobs are the same.

Their jobs as leaders are:

- Clearly define the mission, goals, and vision of the company.

- Find the best people and forge them into a team.

- Strengthen the company on the inside.

- Expand the company on the outside.

- Improve the bottom line.

- Invest in research and development.

- Invest in tangible assets.

- Be a good corporate citizen.

RICH DAD'S
ENTREPRENEURIAL LESSON #9

Don't Fight for the Bargain Basement

Chapter Nine
HOW TO FIND GOOD CUSTOMERS

One day during my junior year of high school, rich dad and I were walking past an entrance to a hotel when we heard a man's voice shouting loudly, "I will not pay you another dime. You have not kept your agreement."

Looking up, I saw a family of five, with a very upset father yelling at a local man in a Hawaiian print shirt. "But all you have paid is a deposit," the local man protested. "You still owe us the balance. I cannot let you check in until the balance is paid. You were to have paid your balance in full a month ago. You're lucky we even held your rooms for you. This is our peak season."

"It's a good thing you did hold our rooms for us," snarled the father. "You'd have heard from my attorney if you hadn't."

"I still need to be paid," said the local man, holding his ground.

"I told you that I will pay you. Don't you have ears? Just check us in, and I will pay you," the father growled. "I have a check right here made out to you. Let us get into our room, and we will settle this once and for all." (This was the era before credit cards.)

"You need to pay in cash. A check will not do. That is why we ask you to pay in full, in advance. It gives us time to clear a personal check."

"What is wrong with you?" asked the father, now shouting at the top of his lungs. "Don't you people understand English? I told you I would pay you. Now show us to our room. Do I have to call your boss to get things done?"

A crowd started to gather. Not wanting to make a scene, the man in the Hawaiian shirt picked up the mountain of suitcases, loaded them on a trolley and directed the family to their room.

"He'll never get paid," said rich dad as we continued.

"How do you know?" I asked.

"We dealt with the same guy three years ago. He did the same thing to us. He's going to go to the room, write the check, and then stop payment on it."

"What happened after he stopped payment?" I asked.

"By the time we found out his check was no good, he had already checked out. We called him once he was back on the mainland—I believe they live in California—and we tried to collect."

"Then what happened?"

"When we threatened to take him to court, he agreed to pay us half of what he owed. He said our service was bad, and he felt he was paying us what we deserved. He said he was being generous paying 50% of what he owed us. Since it would have cost more to take him to court, we agreed. Even then, it was six months before he paid anything."

We walked for a while in silence. Disturbed, I finally had to ask, "Is this common in business?"

"Yes, unfortunately it is. You will always have good customers and bad customers. Fortunately, I have found about 80% of all customers are good customers, 5% are like him—just horrible—and the other 15% are in between," replied rich dad. "Oh, on top of that, this same guy had the nerve to call again last year and try to book a tour package with us. What nerve!"

"Did you do business with him?"

"Are you kidding?" laughed rich dad. "I had already fired him. Our reservation department had his picture and his name on our Do not do business with again list. The person taking the call remembered his name, and told him we were full." (This was before computers which keep track of customers today.)

"You fire customers?" I asked in surprise.

"Absolutely," said rich dad. "You fire bad customers just as you would fire a bad employee. If you do not get rid of your bad employees, the good employees will leave. If I do not fire bad customers, not only will my good customers leave, but many of my good employees will leave as well."

"But aren't some of the complaints or upsets your fault, too?" I asked. "Couldn't the complaints be legitimate?"

"Yes," replied rich dad. "Often it is our fault. Our staff does make mistakes or may offend customers. Our systems can break down. That is why we look into every complaint and take it seriously. Just as you look both ways before you cross a street, when it comes to complaints, we have to look both ways—at the customer and at our operations."

"Is it hard firing people?" I asked. Being 17 years old at the time, the thought of firing someone, especially an adult, frightened me. It was not something I wanted to do.

"It's never pleasant," said rich dad. "It's one of the more unpleasant, yet important jobs of an entrepreneur. Your job is a people job. People are your biggest assets and biggest liabilities. One day you'll have to fire someone. I am sure it will be an experience you will never forget."

Rich dad and I entered a restaurant and found a table to have lunch. Once the waitress had filled our water glasses, handed us the menu, and explained the specials, rich dad continued with his lesson on people. "The same is true with advisors. You must be able to fire bad advisors. If you have accountants or attorneys who do a poor job, or if the job is too big for them, or if they are only interested in receiving their fees and not helping your business, your business will suffer. If you do not get rid of bad advisors, you are responsible. The ultimate price of bad advice is far more than what you pay your advisors in fees for good advice. I had one accountant give me bad tax advice, and it cost me nearly $60,000 in back taxes and penalties. On top of that, it cost me another $12,000 to hire another accounting firm to straighten out the mess. In addition, this mistake upset me so much that I was not effective for months and the business suffered as a result. So as an entrepreneur, you must realize that you are responsible for your own mistakes, as well as for the mistakes of others."

"Were you angry at your accountant?" I asked.

"Yes and no. I really could not blame him. At the time, my business was growing so fast, I did not pay attention to the quality of my advisors. At the time, I did not realize that all accountants are not created equal. He should have told me he did not know what he was doing, but he didn't want to admit it. He was afraid I would fire him. Soon the size of my business was too big for his expertise. He was in over his head. I should have let him go earlier, but I was too busy. Besides, I liked the guy and I knew his family. I kept hoping he would grow with the company. Unfortunately, he didn't. Finally, I did let him go, but only after the losses from his bad advice were very high. So I don't blame him. I'm the only one ultimately responsible for the business. As the business grows, your advisors need to grow with you or go. I learned a valuable lesson."

"Was it hard firing him?" I asked.

"It was extremely difficult. If you cannot hire and fire people, including yourself, you should not be an entrepreneur. Remember this: Your success or failure as an entrepreneur depends a lot on your people skills. If you have strong people skills, your business will grow. If you have poor people skills, your business will suffer. If you hire people simply because you like them or because they are relatives, and you cannot fire them when they need to go, then you have poor people skills. Remember that people are different, and as an entrepreneur, you need to be flexible enough to work with different types of people—people with different skills, ambitions, dreams, behavior, and experiences. If you cannot work with different types of people, once again your business will suffer."

"That is why you always said to Mike and me, 'A leader's job is to get people to work as a team.'"

"That could be your most important job. Remember that departments of a business attract different types of people. For example, salespeople are different from administrative people. They are very different people, almost opposites, and you need to treat them as opposites. For example, never ask an administrative person to hire a salesperson. Instead of hiring a hard-charging salesperson who loves busting down doors, the administrative person will prefer to hire a nice, calm salesperson whose only sales experience was working as a checkout clerk at the supermarket. Also, the administrative person would want to make sure the person enjoyed filling out forms and doing paperwork."

"Why would they do that?" I asked.

"Because birds of a feather flock together. Administrative people think that paperwork is the most important part of the sale. They have no experience in knowing how hard it is to get that sale. You'll see once you get into the real world. In general, salespeople don't like administrative people. Why? Because in general, salespeople hate paperwork, and administrative people are terrified of selling. So don't try to make a top-flight salesperson into a file clerk, or ask a file clerk to become a flamboyant salesperson."

"So is that where most of the friction lies?" I asked. "Between sales and administration?"

"Oh, no," said rich dad emphatically. "A business is one big ball of friction. It is a working model of human conflict. It is a melting pot of egos that is always boiling. When you look at the B-I Triangle™, you will understand why. A business is a blending of different people, different temperaments, different talents, different education, different ages, sexes, and races. Every day when you come to work, most of your problems will be people problems. A salesman made promises the company cannot keep. The customer is irate. Your attorney will not agree with your accountants. Assembly-line workers will not agree with the engineers who designed the assembly line. Management is at war with labor. Technical people are fighting with creative people. Analytical people do not get along with "people" people. College-educated people feel they're smarter than people who did not go to college. Add to this interoffice politics, or worse, sexual affairs within the company, and you will never need to watch TV again. In most cases, a business does not need a competitor. A normal business has so many competitors inside the business, it's amazing that anyone gets any work done at all."

"So that is why an entrepreneur needs to know when to fire someone. If one person upsets the balance, the whole business can boil over because the internal friction gets too great."

"Exactly," smiled rich dad. "I'm sure you see it in your classrooms at school every day. You can already see the different characters in your classmates."

I smiled and said, "And on my football team, my baseball team, and even in band class."

"That is why every team has a coach, a band has a conductor, and every business has a leader. A leader's job is to turn people into teams. One of the reasons so many people are self-employed or own businesses that stay small is that the leader is either not competent with dealing with people, or simply does not want to learn to deal with so many different people. Business and making money would be easy if it were not for people."

The waitress returned to take our order. After she left, rich dad continued, "Let me give you three tips I have learned about dealing with people in business. Tip number one is what I call 'the pain-in-the-ass factor.' That means all people have skills and talents, and are also pains in the ass. I do not care who they are, they have all three—including me. If their pain-in-the-ass factor exceeds their skills and talents, it is time for them to go or to move them to another part of the business."

Chuckling, I said, "Maybe someday you'll earn a Nobel Prize for the pain-in-the-ass factor."

"I should," said rich dad. "Every person in the world who deals with people will stand and applaud me."

"And what is tip number two?" I asked.

"Learn to hire slow and fire fast," said rich dad. "Take the hiring of people very seriously and slowly. Screen them carefully. And if it is time to let them go, do it quickly. Too many managers allow people too many chances. If you can't fire them for some reason, then move them and isolate them. Don't let them contaminate the rest of the people in the business. Maybe you can help them find jobs at a company where they might be happier and more productive. Or just pay them to leave. It will be less expensive in the long run. Remember to do it humanely and legally. All people need to be treated with the appropriate dignity. Many times, when I have let people go, they were happy to move on. I have found that if people are acting up or underperforming, it is not because they are lazy. Many are simply unhappy for a number of reasons. If you as a leader can find a way to make them happy, find it."

"You mean a person can be a good employee, but be working in the wrong job or department?"

"It happens all the time," said rich dad. "In fact, I have been the person who took a good employee and put him in the wrong job. I'm the person who made him unhappy."

"What did you do?"

"Well, years ago, I had this young man who was a great salesperson. He worked hard, treated his customers well, and made the company and himself a lot of money. So, after a few years, I rewarded him by promoting him to sales manager. I put him in charge of 12 other salespeople. He was fine for about a year, but then he began to come to work late, the sales numbers fell, and the sales team was unhappy."

"Did you fire him?"

"No. I was going to, but I thought it would be better to re-interview him again. Once we sat down and had a heart-to-heart talk, I found the problem. By promoting him, I had turned him into an administrative person doing exactly what he hated doing—paperwork. Oh, sure, he had a fancy title, VP of Sales. He made more money and had a company car, but he hated the mountains of paperwork and attending meeting after meeting. He simply wanted to be out on the street, talking to his customers."

"So did he go back to sales?"

"Absolutely! Good salespeople are hard to find. So I gave him a raise, a bigger territory, and he kept the car. He got richer, and so did the company."

"And what is the third lesson?" I asked.

"The third lesson is that there are two kinds of communicators," said rich dad. "When they're upset or unhappy, one type of communicator will come talk to you face to face. They lay the cards on the table in front of you."

"And the second?" I asked,

"The second type stabs you in the back. They gossip, talk badly about you, spread rumors, or complain to everyone else but never to your face.

Basically, these people are cowards. They lack the courage to confront you, to be forthright. Often they will blame you for their lack of courage, saying you are too mean or will not listen or they are afraid of being fired. Their perceptions about you could be true. But generally, these people will choose to talk behind a person's back, rather than face to face. It's just in their nature."

"So how do you handle that?" I asked.

"Well, one way is at every meeting, I remind my staff of the two types of communicators and leave it at that. I say to them, 'There are people who speak to you face to face and there are others who speak behind your back. Which one are you?' Once the rest of the company is aware of the two types, they generally remind someone who is gossiping or stabbing someone in the back about the two types of people. It doesn't totally stop the gossiping, but it does keep it down, and in general, overall communication improves. I also tell them that I would prefer to be stabbed in the chest rather than stabbed in the back. So I don't tell them what to do. I simply give them a choice."

"Have you been stabbed in the chest?" I asked.

"Oh, a number of times—and I deserved it. I needed to be corrected and reminded to be open-minded as much as anyone else. As much as it hurt, it was less destructive than a stab in the back."

"Aren't people afraid of being fired?"

"Oh, there is always that risk," smiled rich dad. "That is why it takes courage and excellent communication skills to be successful in business. In many instances, it is not what you say, but how you say it. So if the communication is going to be unpleasant, put on your creative thinking cap and figure out the most humane and kind way to say what needs to be said. And always remember that communication does not mean talking. Communication also includes listening. When two people are upset and both are talking, friction increases and communication decreases. The reason God gave us two ears and one mouth is to remind us to listen more than speak."

"So being an entrepreneur is a lot about people and the communication skills needed to communicate to them."

Rich dad agreed and continued, saying, "Leadership requires great communication skills. To become a better entrepreneur requires you to focus on improving your communication skills. One of your first steps in your leadership development is to develop the courage to be a face-to-face communicator and to work on developing your communication skills. If you are a stab-them-in-the-back type of communicator, I doubt your business will grow. Entrepreneurship is for people with courage. It's not for cowards. If you will work on always improving your communication skills, your business will grow. Remember that just because you're talking does not mean you're necessarily communicating. And in sales, telling is not selling. Communication is a far more complex process than simply moving your lips and wagging your tongue."

Sitting quietly as rich dad enjoyed his meal, my mind went back to the angry father, the customer whom rich dad had fired. I asked, "And that is why you told that irate customer that you had no vacancies! It was better than telling him what you thought of him."

"Yes. As the entrepreneur, one of your jobs is to protect your company and your employees from cheap customers—the customers who want more than they pay for, the customers who want something for nothing. I had to find a way of firing that customer without getting into an argument again. I knew he would stab me in the back if we got into it. That is why I make it a point to fire cheap customers—politely and discreetly."

"Isn't that cruel or discriminating against poor people?"

"I did not say 'poor' people," said rich dad, raising his voice. "The word I used was *cheap*. Cheap customers, not poor people. There is a difference. There are rich cheap people and poor cheap people. Cheap has nothing to do with money. It has to do with a state of mind. In some cases, I would say it borders on a mental illness. Also, I would not classify cheap people in the same category as bargain hunters. We all love a bargain. Yet as much as we love value for our money, very few of us want value at the expense of someone else. But a cheap person does. A cheap person borders on being a thief, and sometimes they are thieves. If it's not money they're stealing, they steal your time and your energy. They steal your peace of mind.

"For all the months of misery that that one guy caused our company, it would have been better for us to let him just stay for free. He sucked the life out of our business for months. He seemed to enjoy messing with us. He always changed the deal and said we said things we did not say. He always wanted a better price, even after he agreed to pay a set price. He seemed to enjoy having us come after him. Instead of spending time on our good customers, we spent time on him. Having a bad customer can cost us good customers. That is why I say that you need to fire your cheap customers. They're too expensive. This is a very important lesson to learn if you want to be an entrepreneur. Always remember, take very good care of your good customers, and fire your cheap customers."

How to Find Good Customers

In business, a very important word is the word *margin*. It is as important a term as *cash flow*. In fact, both terms are intricately related. In overly simple terms, *margin* is the difference between what it costs to produce your product and the price you sell your product for. For example, let's say it costs you two dollars to manufacture your widget, and you sell your widget for ten dollars. In this case, your gross margin is eight dollars. There are three reasons why a product's gross margin is so important.

1. **The gross margin finances the rest of the B-I Triangle™.**
   Looking at the B-I Triangle, you can see that a product's margin must provide enough cash flow to feed the rest of the Triangle.

Margin pays for the team's salaries, legal fees, the company's system operations, marketing, and accounting. These are also known as operating expenses.

2. **Margin determines the price of your product.**
   Obviously, the more margin, the higher the price of your product.

3. **Product and price determine your customer.**
   To help clarify this, let's look at the automobile industry. A Rolls-Royce is known as a very expensive car. It attracts a certain type of customer. If Rolls-Royce suddenly announced it was going to produce a low-priced budget model, many of their rich customers would probably start looking for another brand of car.

Wrong Car, Wrong Price, Wrong Customer

Recently, Jaguar announced it was dropping its lower-priced model because it realized that offering a lower-priced model had hurt its sales. After losing $700 million in one year, they finally realized that they should stay at the high end of the car market and not try to capture market share in the mid-price market.

Today, many brands are made in the same factory. For example, a factory that produces blue jeans can produce jeans for a high-end brand and a low-end brand. It is basically the same product, but the high-end brand can command a higher price and is sold through a different distribution channel, let's say Saks Fifth Avenue. If the high-end brand wants to produce a low-end brand, they had best create another brand for a different distribution channel, let's say Walmart. In fact, that is what many big companies do. They produce the same product, but under different brands representing different price points for different customers.

So to find good customers, you need to match the product and the price to fit the customer's needs, wants, and ego. In many cases, the customer's ego is far more important than wants and needs.

How Much Is Your Product Worth?

In 1996 after the *CASHFLOW*® game was in its final production and ready for commercial use, the next question was: How much is this game worth? How much can we sell the game for? Those of you who have seen our game may recognize some of the challenges we faced. When Kim and I first saw our finished, commercial version of the game for the first time, both of us were as proud as new parents. We were also concerned. The packaging looked great, but we thought it might have looked too much like a game for entertainment rather than education. We made it look bright and fun because we wanted learning to be fun. But as we looked at our finished product, we began to wonder: How much would someone pay for fun?

We wanted people to know the game was about education, but again, how much would someone pay for education? Looking at our finished product for the first time, Kim and I knew we had serious marketing challenges.

To find out what the market might think about our product, once again, we formed a group of people who did not know us, as we did with the beta test, and asked them what they thought of the packaging. The feedback was mixed, from "It looks great," to "It looks stupid." The people in the group did not know we were the creators of the game, so their opinions were pretty frank, often painful.

Next, we asked them what they thought the price of the game should be. Again, not knowing us or what went into creating a game and not having played the game, the prices they suggested ranged from $19.95 to a high of $39.95. This was even more depressing. At that point in time, due to the small production runs, our cost just for producing the game, without freight, was forty-six dollars per game. This did not include the development costs. We were starting off with a product with a negative margin, before we added in the costs of the rest of the B-I Triangle™. When I was manufacturing my nylon wallets, a joke among manufacturers was, "Even if I am losing two dollars a unit, we're going to make it up on volume."

Calling In a Consultant

We called in a consultant to the toy industry who had expertise with board games. After trying the game himself, he gave us his opinion of *CASHFLOW*®. His first comment was, "The game is too difficult." He said, "People have become less smart. If *Monopoly*® were introduced today, it would be rejected too because it would be deemed too difficult. Today, games must be so simple that all the instructions on how to play the game can be understood within a couple of minutes."

We also asked him how much we could sell the game for. He replied, "You might get thirty-nine dollars at retail. That means you would have to sell it to a retail store for twenty dollars, even less if you sell it to a major chain such as Walmart. You might have to sell it for as low as ten dollars just to get it into a store.

"On top of that, if you do get it into a store, you'll have a bigger problem with customers who return the product. They might buy the game for fun because your packaging is fun and place it with their other games. But when they find out how hard it is to play and that it is educational, many of them will return the game to the store and ask for their money back. You could find yourselves with huge losses from refunds and damaged returned games."

Looking for New Answers

It was obvious that our game was not meant for the public market. We knew the game was not for everyone. We knew the game was intended for anyone who thought his or her financial education was important. The problem was to find that customer in the sea of people.

The game was also hard to categorize by demographics. For example, if we had written a book for children, placing the book would be easy. We could place it anywhere parents shopped for kids. But this game could be played by anyone, from kids to adults, male or female.

It was also for people whether they were rich or poor, just as long as they valued their financial education. And we knew our customers would want to be financially proactive. After teaching entrepreneurship and investing for years, I knew that most people wanted more money, but very few people would actually take the time to learn about how to make more money. The challenge was to find the customer who would want the educational game and the information locked within it.

At a marketing seminar, I learned a guideline known as the five P's. These are the five things a marketer must know when selling a product. I believe they were identified by E. Jerome McCarthy. They are:

1. Product

2. Person

3. Price

4. Place

5. Position

A marketer must know what the product is, the person who wants the product, what price they are willing to pay, where the product will be placed so the customer can find it, and how to position it in the marketplace—that is, the biggest, the smallest, the first, the last, and so on.

Entrepreneurs should enjoy solving business problems and normally I do, but this problem had me stumped. All I had were the first two P's. One day a friend called to say he was coming to Phoenix to go to a special seminar on marketing and wanted to know if I wanted to go along. I jumped at the chance.

The room was filled with approximately 300 people, and by the look of them, most seemed to be entrepreneurs. Not too many had the corporate look. The instructor was a wild man who talked about how advertising agencies just waste your money on expensive, good-looking ads or TV spots that sell nothing, a point of view I agreed with. He said, "The purpose of marketing is to get the phone to ring. With these ad agencies, the only phone that rings is them calling to ask you for more money to buy more advertising, so they can collect more fees. Ask them if they can guarantee your sales or measure your sales. In most cases they cannot or will not guarantee their work. All they want to do is win awards for creative advertising for their agency—with your advertising dollars."

Sales = Income

The seminar was exactly what I was looking for. It was marketing for entrepreneurs, not big corporations with millions in advertising dollars to spend. The instructor had a great track record for success and told stories that came from real-life experiences. Some of the other points he made were:

- The entrepreneur must be the best salesperson in his or her business.

- The entrepreneur must be the best marketer in his or her business.

- The marketing efforts must produce sales, not just good-looking ads or slick commercials.

As obvious as these points are, you would be surprised how many entrepreneurs delegate those important roles to ad agencies. Ad agencies are generally for big corporations or established businesses. In a small start-up business, the entrepreneur needs to be the best they can be at sales and marketing. With limited resources, every dollar spent must result in sales—because sales equal income.

Rich dad drummed into my head: "Sales = Income." He would also say, the reason so many people have low incomes is that they are poor at selling. If he had been at this sales seminar, he would have loved it. The instructor was adamant about using marketing that leads to sales that can be proven and measured.

Toward the end of the day, I got the marketing answer I was looking for. When discussing how to price a product, the instructor said, "There are three price points for any product—the lowest-priced, the highest-priced, and the middle-priced. The worst price to be is the middle price. Nobody knows who you are. The trouble with being the lowest-priced product is that someone is always trying to beat you. Someone will find a way to sell the same product for less than you do. To win the lowest-price competition, you have to make less and less money. On top of that, you have to deal with cheap customers."

With that statement, the pieces of the puzzle began to come together. Immediately, I remembered the conversation I had had with rich dad years earlier about cheap customers. Bringing my thoughts back into the seminar, the instructor roared on about why being the most expensive was the best position to fight for. He said, "When I was a struggling marketing consultant, I tried to keep my prices low. The problem was, the lower I made my prices, the cheaper my customers became. Soon, instead of selling my services, I was spending more time haggling about my fees with cheap customers. When I raised my fees a little, I joined the masses of other middle-of-the-road marketing consultants. Again, most of my time was spent discussing price rather than the value of my product, what I could do for the customer. Then one day, I decided to be ridiculous and simply raise my fees to the highest in my industry. Instead of charging $50 an hour for my services, I raised my rates to $25,000 per day. Today I work less, earn far more money, and work with a better class of client."

My mind raced when I heard his fee of $25,000 per day. I realized that I was the cheap client he did not want. Once I got over the shock of realizing I was the cheap one, I began to see that it was my own cheapness that was causing me to struggle at pricing my board game. I was looking at price rather than the value of the game.

"Don't fight for the bargain basement," boomed the instructor. "The bargain basement attracts cheap customers."

Once again my mind drifted off, recalling how rich dad hated dealing with people who were cheap. Rich dad said, "Design your product and its price for a very special customer. Your marketing should then find ways of reaching that special customer. Be creative. Don't be cheap. The bargain basement is not a place to find good customers."

The Book Takes Priority

That evening, I went home and talked with Kim. The first thing I said was, "We should sell the board game for $200. We will position it as the most expensive game in the world. It's not just a game. It's a seminar in a box."

Kim agreed. She did not flinch at the idea of selling a board game for that much money, even if our focus group said it should sell for $39.95.

I continued, "Our problem is that we have been asking the opinion of people who will probably never be our customers. We have been asking for the opinion of people who shop in the bargain basement, not in the boardroom. We need to find customers who value education and are willing to pay for it."

"We'll need a way to find them," Kim added.

"The book takes priority. Instead of focusing on marketing the game, we will begin to focus on marketing the book. The book will help us find our customers. The book will become our company brochure." At the time, I was working on *Rich Dad Poor Dad*.

"So we need to weave the game into the book," Kim said. "And we go back on the road doing investment seminars, working with the same type of customer we have been working with for years."

"That's the idea. We finish the book, and we get back on the road doing seminars for people who pay for financial education. We've been doing it for years. It's a low-risk idea. We know the business and we know how to reach those customers.

"In other words, the tactic remains the same. The sole tactic of the business is to get people to play the *CASHFLOW*® game. We now focus on the strategies. If the strategies work, people will play the game."

Kim and I were in agreement. We were a team with a unified plan.

"So why $200?" asked Kim. "How did you come up with that number?"

"It took a while," I said. "But when the instructor said, 'A higher price can be perceived as more valuable,' the lights in my head went on. I realized I was cheap and looking at my own product through cheap eyes, rather than looking at the value hidden in the game. So I went up to $59 a game, and that still sounded cheap. I was now in the middle, not at the top. In my mind, I then tested $99 a game. I was comfortable with that. I knew I could sell it at that price so I knew I had not yet reached the top. When I tried $200 in my head, I felt uncomfortable. Now I knew I had gone beyond my own comfort level. I had found my price."

"Well, it certainly gives us a large margin. That will help us grow the business," said Kim. "So we market the book through traditional distribution channels. That handles the place category of the five P's— where we place our product in front of potential customers. Instead of trying to drop the price of the game to fit into that distribution channel, we can use a conventionally priced book and flow it through the book-distribution system. That way, the book will sell the game, or at least help us find customers. And the seminars will sell the game," Kim summarized. "But there is still something else behind charging $200 a game."

"Well," I began slowly, "if we compare games to games, the game is not worth $200. But when compared as education to education, the game is really inexpensive. Just look at how much a college education costs in both time and money. On top of that, you don't learn much about money or investing in school. Also look at how much it costs for people to lose money in the stock market. That is even more expensive. But the biggest expense of all is the loss of opportunity. So many people want to invest and know they should invest, but they fail to invest simply because they lack the financial education. Not only can this game help a person make millions of dollars, but it can also help a person become financially free."

"But what about the people who might feel ripped off at $200?" asked Kim.

"Many people will, and they may never buy the game," I replied. "If we price the game at $200, people will have to think long and hard about the value of the game before they buy it. And that is what we want them to do. We want the price to make them think about value more than just entertainment."

"And just think of the number of people one game can reach. One $200 game can reach hundreds of people," added Kim. "Not everyone has to buy the game."

"And that is why the sole tactic of our company is to have people play the game—not necessarily buy the game," I replied. "People who are serious about their education and pay $200 for the game will be more likely to take the time to learn the game. The only way they can learn the game is to invite others to play. The game immediately begins to fulfill its mission. The more people who play the game and invite other people to play the game, the more the cost per player goes down—and the value of the game goes up. Our only job now is to find that person who values education and is willing to pay for it.

"We also make the game harder to get, harder for people to find. We will have to be smarter about letting people know how to find us through our website," I added. "By keeping access to the game more restricted instead of using mass-marketing, we will highlight its educational value. Our focus groups were looking at it as a mass-market game, not as the educational tool that it is."

"And what happens if it doesn't work?" asked Kim.

"Then we come up with more ideas," I replied. "Ideas are plentiful if you're creative. Our strategies are low-risk. With the book and the seminars, we should have cash flow from those two strategies so we do not need to sell as many games. In this way, we give the game the opportunity to sell itself, to find its own fans and its own channels of distribution. If it is a valuable product, the plan will work. If our customers do not find the game valuable, we shut the business down. Only time will tell."

As stated earlier, the first time the game was played commercially was at an investment seminar in Las Vegas, Nevada, in November 1996. In February 2004, when I saw the nearly full-page article in the *New York Times*, I knew the game had found its rightful audience.

We have now sold hundreds of thousands of games, and there are CASHFLOW clubs all over the world meeting regularly to play the game. We have very few complaints about its price. Our return factor is less than one percent. We found the right customers for the game.

Develop Your Marketing Plan

The five P's are a simple guideline for your marketing plan. Before you quit your job, remember these important points.

1. There are three price positions in any market—the highest price, the middle price, and the lowest price. Decide which price best fits you. Always remember that the middle price may be the most comfortable, but it is also the most crowded. It's hard to be outstanding if you're average.

2. The lowest-price leaders do not just lower their price. The winners in the lowest-price category do something brilliant in business that their competitors cannot do. For example, Walmart sells the same products many other retailers sell, but Walmart has a far better system of retailing that allows them to make a lot of money with smaller margins. Remember what rich dad said, "Any idiot can drop their price and go broke. It takes a brilliant business person to drop their prices, cut their margins, and get rich." He also said, "If you choose to compete at the low end of the market, you have to be a better businessman than those who compete at the top." Since I am not that good a businessperson, I find it easier to compete at the top.

3. If you are going to be the highest-price product in your market niche, then you have to give your customers something your competitors cannot give. If you are confused by what high-priced businesses do, then do your homework. Go to a high-priced auto dealer, and then go to a low-priced auto dealer. Or go to a high-priced hotel, and then go to a budget hotel. By taking notice of differences, you find ways of better defining your product and your customer. Know that the higher the price, the fewer the customers and the more precise you need to be in your marketing. Also, never ask people who shop in the bargain basements of the world what they think of a Rolls-Royce.

4. Don't try to be all things to all customers. If you want the high end and the low end, start two brands. As you know, Honda has its Acura brand and Toyota has its Lexus brand. To me, they look like the same cars, but what do I know? Obviously, the marketers at Honda and Toyota have done a good job convincing the public that they are selling two different cars. As stated earlier in this chapter, marketing needs to fill a customer's wants, needs, and ego. In many cases, ego has more buying power.

5. Instead of discounting down, bonus up. I know people look at the game and flinch at the price. Rather than drop the price, we prefer to add products to the mix and then increase the price of the package. As rich dad said, "Sales=Income." So rather than cut our price and reduce our margins, which anyone can do, we would rather find ways of keeping our prices while increasing the value and having a satisfied customer.

6. Weak salespeople always want new products to sell. When I was at Xerox, it was always the weakest sales reps who said, "If we had new products, I could sell more." Many businesses fall into this trap. When sales are down, they look for new products, which often leads to a phenomenon known as "line extension." When line extension happens too much, the customer can become confused because there are too many products to choose from, and your own products can become your competitors. Rich dad said, "Instead of looking for new products to sell, look for new customers." He also said, "A smart entrepreneur focuses on keeping existing customers happy and looking for new customers to sell existing products to."

7. Look for strategic partners who already sell to the customer you want to sell to. Earlier in this book, I wrote about the three kinds of money: competitive, cooperative, and spiritual. One of the ways to become richer faster with less risk is to be cooperative and earn cooperative money.

8. Treat your best customers well. The Internet makes keeping in touch with your best customers easier than ever. The rule of thumb is: Focus on keeping your best customers happy, because not only will they buy more from you, but they will also tell their friends about you. That is the best kind of marketing of all. It's called *word of mouth*. When it comes to taking care of your best customers, be creative. One of the reasons small entrepreneurial companies beat the big corporations is simply because a small company can be more creative and be more creative faster.

In Summary

Always remember the five P's. Remember that your very special product is important to a very special person.

The price of your product must satisfy the person's needs, wants, and ego. When it comes to ego, we all like finding a bargain. Also, many of us like letting people know we spent a lot of money for a product that only a few people can or will afford. So ego can work at the high end as well as the low end.

Where you place your product so your customer can find it is important. Always remember that a new Ferrari will look out of place in a used-car lot filled with cheap cars. If you place your product in the wrong place, your sales will suffer. When *Rich Dad Poor Dad* was first printed, we placed the book in our friend's car wash/gas station in Texas. Why that car wash? Because that was the place where the affluent people brought their cars for a wash and for gas. If we had put our book in a place were people came to buy cheap gas, I believe the books would still be there.

The only position you want to be in is in first position. Always remember that most of us know that Lindbergh was the first human to fly solo nonstop across the Atlantic. Very few people know who was second. If you are not first in your category, then invent a new category you can be the first in. When the game was not known, we became the first game to claim the highest-priced-game category. When Avis realized it was second to Hertz, it took first place by being first to claim to be proud of being in second place, which led to their "We Try Harder" slogan.

In conclusion, the most important place you want to be first in is in your customers' minds. For example, when you think of a soft drink, do you first think of Coca-Cola® or Pepsi®? When your very special customers think of your product category, do they think of you first or your competitor first? Ultimately, the most important job of an entrepreneur is to be first in the mind of your customers.

RICH DAD'S
ENTREPRENEURIAL LESSON #10
Know When to Quit

Chapter Ten

THE SUMMARY

Knowing When to Quit

The fact that you don't like your job is not a good reason to become an entrepreneur. It may sound like a good reason, but it is not a strong enough reason. It definitely lacks a strong enough mission. Although almost everyone can become an entrepreneur, entrepreneurship is not for everyone.

There is an old saying that goes, "Winners never quit and quitters never win." Personally, I do not agree with that saying. It is too simple. In my reality, a winner also knows when to quit. Sometimes in life, it is best to cut your losses. It is best to admit you have come to a dead end or to admit you have been barking up the wrong tree.

In my opinion, a quitter is someone who quits simply because things have gotten tough. I have been a quitter many times in my life. I have quit diet programs, exercise programs, girlfriends, businesses, books, studies, and so on. Every year I make New Year's resolutions and quit. So I know what quitting is and that I am a quitter.

One of the reasons I did not quit my process in becoming an entrepreneur was that I really wanted to be one. I wanted it badly. I wanted to enjoy the freedom, the independence, the wealth, and the ability to make a contribution to this world that a successful entrepreneur has. In spite of how badly I wanted to become a successful entrepreneur, the powerful concept of quitting was always right in front of me, holding the door open. It would have been easy to quit when I was out of money and owed a lot of money. It would have been easy to quit every time a creditor demanded payment. It would have been easy to quit when the tax department let me know that I owed more in back taxes. It would have been easy to quit when a project failed or a potential partner walked out of the deal. When things were tough, quitting was always lurking nearby, just a handshake away.

For me, becoming an entrepreneur is a process, a process I am still in. I believe I will be an entrepreneur in training till the end. I love business and I love solving business problems. There have been times I have cut my losses, shut a business down, and changed directions, but when it came to the process of becoming an entrepreneur, I have never quit—at least not yet. It is a process I love. It is a process that brings me the kind of life I want. So although the process has been tough for me, it has been worth it.

Even though it was tough for me, that does not mean it needs to be tough for you. One reason for writing this book is that I want to make the process easier for anyone who is about to start the process or is already in the process.

Before ending this book, I thought I would leave you with one little thing that kept me going. It was the glow in the dark, even in the darkest of hours. I had a little piece of paper taped to the base of the telephone in my office at the wallet company. That little piece of paper came from a Chinese fortune cookie. It said, "You can always quit. Why start now?" There were many phone calls I had to handle that provided me with more than enough reason to quit. Yet after hanging up the phone, I would glance at the words of wisdom from the fortune cookie and say to myself, "As much as I want to quit, I won't quit today. I'll quit tomorrow." The good thing is, tomorrow never came.

Before You Quit Your Job, I Offer These Tips

- **Check your attitude.**

  Attitude is almost everything. We don't recommend becoming an entrepreneur just to make money. There are far easier ways to make money. If you do not love business and the challenges a business offers, then entrepreneurship may not be for you.

- **Get as much experience as possible on all five levels of the B-I Triangle™.**

  In earlier books, we advised people to work to learn, not work to earn. Instead of taking jobs for the money, take jobs for the experience. For example, if you want to gain experience in how business systems work, get a part-time job at McDonald's. You would be surprised at what happens the moment a customer says, "I want a Big Mac and fries." The moment that happens, one of the world's best-designed business systems takes over. It is a brilliantly designed system run primarily by people with only a high school education.

- **Always remember that Sales = Income.**

  All entrepreneurs need to be good in sales. If you are not good in sales, get as much experience as possible before you quit your job. I heard Donald Trump once say, "Some people are born salespeople. The rest of us can learn to sell." I am not a natural salesperson. I did train hard to become one. If you want really great sales training, you may want to consider joining a network-marketing business or a direct-sales business.

- **Be optimistic as well as brutally honest with yourself.**

  In his book, *Good to Great*, Jim Collins does an excellent piece on this need to be brutally honest. He writes about his interviews with Admiral Stockwell, one of the longest-held POWs from the Vietnam War. When Jim Collins asked the admiral which type of person died in their cells, the admiral answered without hesitation, "The optimists." The POWs who did survive were those who could handle the brutal facts about their situation. On the flip side, know the difference between being brutally honest and being pessimistic. I know people who will tell you why something will not work even if it's working. I know people who store in their mind every piece of negative news possible. Negative people, or pessimistic people, are not the same as brutally honest people.

- **Do you know how to spend money?**
  Too many people struggle financially because they do not know how to spend their money. Too many people spend their money, and it never comes back. An entrepreneur needs to know how to spend money and have more money come back. It is not about being cheap, tight, or frugal. It's about knowing when to spend, what to spend on, and how much to spend. I have seen too many entrepreneurs go broke saving money. For example, when business drops off, instead of spending money on more promotions, some entrepreneurs cut back hoping to save money. When this happens, business continues to drop off. This is an example of the wrong action at the wrong time.

- **Start a business to practice on.**
  No one can learn to ride a bicycle without a bicycle, and no one can learn to start, build, and run a business without a business. Once you are familiar with the different parts of the B-I Triangle™, stop planning and start doing. As I have always said, "Keep your full-time job, and start a part-time business."

- **Be willing to ask for help.**
  Rich dad often said, "Arrogance is the cause of ignorance." If you don't know something, ask someone who does know. On the flip side, don't be a pest and ask for too much help. There is a fine line between help and a crutch.

- **Find a mentor.**
  Rich dad was my mentor. I have had many other mentors. Read books about great entrepreneurs such as Edison, Ford, and Gates. Books can be your best mentors. One of my favorite entrepreneurs is Steve Jobs, founder of Apple and Pixar. Not only do I like his style, but I love the culture of his business. One of the most

important things an entrepreneur can build is a business with a strong culture. As stated earlier, The Rich Dad Company works hard to foster and protect a culture of learning and free expression.

- **Join an entrepreneur's network.**
  Birds of a feather do flock together. Every city I have ever lived in has groups or associations of entrepreneurs. Attend their meetings and find one that fits your needs. Surround yourself with fellow entrepreneurs. They are there for support as well as to be supported. Contact your SBA, the Small Business Administration, or your local chamber of commerce for a schedule of meetings and seminars. They are great sources of information as well as resources for entrepreneurs. One group I have been impressed with is YEO, the Young Entrepreneurs Organization. Although I am too old to belong to this group of young men and women, I have been asked to speak at several of their chapters. I have always been impressed with the quality of young person this organization attracts.

- **Be faithful to the process.**
  One reason why many people do not quit their jobs and become entrepreneurs is that entrepreneurship can be extremely challenging, especially when first starting out. I suggest you follow the basics of the B-I Triangle™ and diligently do your best to master all eight categories of the Triangle. It takes time, but if you are successful, the rewards can be immense. As rich dad said, "Entrepreneurship is a process, not a job or profession." So be faithful to the process and remember that even when times are bad, the process will give you a glimpse of the future that lies ahead.

Over the years I have heard many people use the term *BHAG*, which stands for "Big Hairy Audacious Goal." While having a big hairy goal is commendable, I believe the process and the size of the mission are more important than the goal.

Rich dad drew a diagram for his son and me that looked like this:

MISSION $\longrightarrow$ PROCESS $\longrightarrow$ GOAL

He said, "If you are going to have a big goal, you need a strong mission to push you through the process. With a strong mission, anything is attainable."

Thank you for reading this book. I wish you the best of success in your journey as an entrepreneur.

—Robert Kiyosaki

About the Author
Robert Kiyosaki

Best known as the author of *Rich Dad Poor Dad*—the #1 personal finance book of all time—Robert Kiyosaki has challenged and changed the way tens of millions of people around the world think about money. He is an entrepreneur, educator, and investor who believes the world needs more entrepreneurs who will create jobs.

With perspectives on money and investing that often contradict conventional wisdom, Robert has earned an international reputation for straight talk, irreverence, and courage and has become a passionate and outspoken advocate for financial education.

Robert and Kim Kiyosaki are founders of The Rich Dad Company, a financial education company, and creators of the *CASHFLOW*® games. In 2013, the company will leverage the global success of the Rich Dad games in the launch of a new and breakthrough offering in mobile and online gaming.

Robert has been heralded as a visionary who has a gift for simplifying complex concepts. He has shared his personal journey to financial freedom in ways that resonate with audiences of all ages and backgrounds. His core principles and messages—like "Your house is not an asset," "Invest for cash flow," and his predictions in *Rich Dad's Prophecy*—ignited a firestorm of criticism and ridicule, only to have played out on the world economic stage over the past decade in ways that were both unsettling and prophetic.

His point of view is that "old" advice—go to college, get a good job, save money, get out of debt, invest for the long term, and diversify— has become obsolete advice in today's fast-paced Information Age. His Rich Dad philosophies and messages challenge the status quo. His teachings encourage people to become financially educated and to take an active role in investing for their future.

Money Doesn't Make You Rich –
Your Financial IQ Does

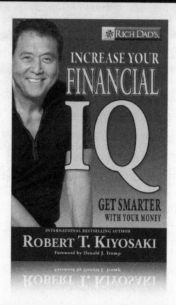

Many think that money makes a person rich. But Robert Kiyosaki explains in
Rich Dad's Increase Your Financial IQ: Get Smarter With Your Money
that money is simply a by-product of your financial IQ.

- Learn and harness the power of the five financial intelligences
- Discover how the mind best learns new information
- Get smarter with your money

Robert provides valuable insight into getting rich drawn from his life's
experiences in investing and business, in this *New York Times* bestseller.

Increase your financial IQ and get smarter with your money with
Rich Dad's Increase Your Financial IQ: Get Smarter With Your Money.

Order your copy at
richdad.com today!